TECHNOLOGY
ACQUISITION

Buying the Future of Your Business

ALLEN ESKELIN

ADDISON-WESLEY

Boston • San Francisco • New York • Toronto • Montreal
London • Munich • Paris • Madrid
Capetown • Sydney • Tokyo • Singapore • Mexico City

The publisher offers discounts on this book when ordered in quantity for special sales. For more information, please contact:

Pearson Education Corporate Sales Division
One Lake Street
Upper Saddle River, NJ 07458
(800) 382-3419
corpsales@pearsontechgroup.com

Visit AW on the Web: www.awl.com/cseng/

Library of Congress Cataloging-in-Publication Data

Eskelin, Allen.
    Technology acquisition : buying the future of your business / Allen Eskelin.
        p. cm.
    Includes bibliographical references and index.
    ISBN 0-201-73804-X
    1. Information technology. 2. Project management. I. Title.

  HC79.I55 E83 2001
  658.7'2—dc21   2001022764

0-201-73804-X
This product is printed digitally on demand.
First printing, June 2001

To Wendy
I Love You

ABOUT THE AUTHOR

Allen Eskelin currently provides information technology leadership to Starbucks Coffee Company in Seattle, Washington. Previously, he managed projects for Gateway 2000 in North Sioux City, South Dakota, as it grew from an $800 million direct marketer of personal computers to an $8 billion global brand. During this time, he managed several successful technology acquisition projects. After reading this book, join Allen at www.technologyacquisition.com to continue the discussion and share your experiences to advance the practice and profession of technology acquisition project management.

Contents

Acknowledgments

I want to thank Wendy Eskelin, my loving wife, who gave me unlimited inspiration and support during the process of writing this book.

Many thanks also go to:

- Steve McConnell, a friend and mentor, who believed in me and helped me accomplish one of my dreams.

- Steve Densford, for his friendship and continued support from the first day I had the idea to write this book. Every writer needs a sounding board. Steve invested at least a hundred cups of Starbucks coffee and countless hours of brainstorming and debate into this book.

- Ron Snyder and Frances White, two good friends who participated in the formal review process to help shape the book and provide important feedback. Thanks as well to all of the others who participated in the review process.

- Peter Gordon, my editor at Addison-Wesley, who kept me pointed in the right direction throughout the process.

- Alicia Carey, Asdis Thorsteinsson, Karin Hansen, Chris Guzikowski, Kate Saliba, Patrick Peterson, and all of Addison-Wesley. Additional thanks to Kathy Glidden of Stratford Publishing Services and Anne Marie Walker.

- Kerby Eskelin for his assistance and support throughout this process.

- Gateway 2000 and Starbucks Coffee Company for providing me the opportunity to exercise and improve this process over many technology acquisition projects.

- All the other writers who have educated and inspired me while continually feeding my passion for books.

Reference Map

The following table is a good starting point for future reference of this book.

Process	People	Tools	Case Studies
Initiation (p. 2)	• Project Sponsor (p. 13) • Project Manager (p. 15) • Project Stakeholders (p. 18)	• Business Need (p. 5) • Project Charter (p. 7)	• Addressing the Wrong Business Need (p. 3) • Communicating the Project Charter (p. 12)
Planning (p. 24)	• Project Team (p. 51)	• Project Plan (p. 25) • Project Schedule (p. 31) • Decision Scoring Matrix (p. 38)	• Unprofessional Team Members (p. 55)
Research (p. 61)	• Vendor Sales Team (p. 119)	• Request for Proposal (p. 72)	
Evaluation (p. 123)			• Surprises That Surface after the Decision (p. 128)
Negotiation (p. 133)	• Negotiation Team (p. 144)	• Negotiation Strategy (p. 139) • Deal Sheet (p. 143)	

continued next page

Process	People	Tools	Case Studies
Implementation (p. 148)	• Internal Implemention Team (p. 152) • Vendor Implementation Team (p. 154)		• Separating Environments (p. 151)
Operation (p. 157)	• Internal Support Team (p. 162) • Vendor Support Team (p. 164) • End Users (p. 165)		

Introduction

A very large number of Information Technology (IT) projects fail every year. Some studies have shown that only one fourth of all IT projects undertaken by Fortune 500 companies are completed successfully. Others give IT projects only a 50 percent chance of being completed within time and cost budgets.

Would you invest millions of dollars in a project with a 25 percent chance of success? IT managers are increasingly answering no to this question. So what is their alternative? Their alternative is to shift this risk to a third party. The risk can be reduced by acquiring technology from outside companies specializing in building technology instead of attempting to build it internally.

The Shift from Building to Buying Technology

There are many trends that are causing IT managers to shift from building to buying technology.

One of these trends is an increase in demand for IT professionals. As technology becomes more critical to all businesses, the need for quality IT professionals increases. This increase in demand has caused the price of these resources to rise to a point where it is much more costly to develop technology in-house than ever before.

One painful consequence of the IT resource shortage is that as demand for IT professionals far exceeds supply, companies are being forced to extend development schedules and limit their growth plans.

Another trend is the increasingly high rate of change in new technology. As growth in technology accelerates, it becomes more difficult to keep up with current technology and remain competitive.

Combine these trends, the high rate of IT project failure, the shortage of IT professionals and its impact on project schedules, and the increasingly high rate of change in technology, and it's no wonder that IT managers are starting to buy instead of build their technology whenever possible.

The Ground Rules

The goal of this book is to describe a way of managing a technology acquisition project that will facilitate the decision-making process so that you select the right vendor, with the right technology, for your business. The book also discusses how to implement and operate the technology once you have selected the vendor.

Early in my career, I managed several software development projects. One day, I was asked to manage a project to acquire technology. I searched everywhere looking for information on how to manage this type of project. I perused bookstores, libraries, magazines, and the Internet looking for anything I could find on the subject. I found many books on the topics of project management, negotiation, outsourcing, software development, government technology acquisition, and business acquisition. But there was nothing that specifically addressed these topics in the context of acquiring technology for a typical business. I was forced to read several books on the topics previously listed in order to extract the information that would help me successfully manage this type of project. I eventually ended up creating my own project life cycle. After applying this project life cycle to several successful technology acquisition projects, I decided to share my findings with other project managers who are faced with the same challenges I faced. I am writing the book I wish I had before managing my first technology acquisition.

I have tried to keep the information presented in this book at a level where it will be most useful to an experienced project manager who is new to managing a technology acquisition project. However, if you have 10 years' experience in managing technology acquisitions, you shouldn't jump to the conclusion that there is nothing here for you.

This is not a book about managing government technology acquisitions or $100 million or more technology acquisitions. An experienced project manager who has never managed a technology acquisition will more than likely *not* get a chance to manage an acquisition of more than $10 million on his first project of this type.

Additionally, a process this extensive would be difficult to justify on an acquisition of less than $500,000. This book is targeted at the experienced project manager who will be, or is, managing his first technology acquisition of $500,000 to $10 million. That said, there is also value for anyone who is involved with a technology acquisition. This includes executive management, IT management, project stakeholders, project sponsors, project teams, vendors, implementation teams, support teams, or any others who are impacted in some way by a technology acquisition project.

As you read this book, you might find that this process is simple. I have elected to outline a step-by-step process that will be simple enough to use in your first technology acquisition project. As you gain experience, you may elect to modify this process or expand it to better fit your situation.

My goal is to help you through the first project successfully while providing you with practical advice and techniques and an understanding of how to deal with the most important ingredient of any project, the people.

The Technology Acquisition Project Life Cycle

Many internal development efforts fail, and many trends are causing a shift from building to buying technology. Due to this increase in the acquisition of technology, there is a need for a project life cycle that project managers can use to manage an acquisition project. Before discussing the project life cycle, a few definitions are in order:

- *Project:* A temporary endeavor undertaken to create a unique product or service (The Project Management Institute, Project Management Body of Knowledge, 2000 Edition).

- *Project life cycle:* The division of a project into phases to provide better management control and appropriate links to ongoing operations of the performing organization. Collectively, the phases are known as the project life cycle (The Project Management Institute, Project Management Body of Knowledge, 2000 Edition).

- *Technology acquisition:* A project undertaken to acquire technology from a third party and implement it within the performing organization.

With these definitions in order, let's move on to discussing a project life cycle for a technology acquisition project.

There are many project life cycles available for the technology development project. These life cycles generally include phases for definition, design, development, testing, implementation, and operations. Figure I-1 illustrates some of the project life cycles for building technology.

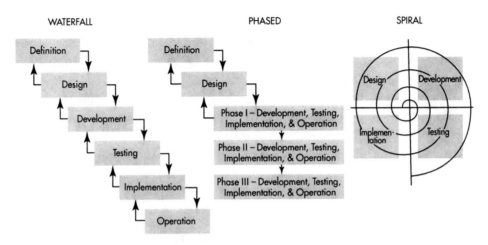

Figure I-1: Development project life cycles

Many of the phases used in a development project are also used in a technology acquisition project. But, there are additional phases needed for a technology acquisition project life cycle to be complete. Although there are many project life cycles available for development projects, there isn't a generally accepted project life cycle for technology acquisition projects. When I was faced with my first technology acquisition project, I was unable to find a project life cycle that specifically addressed this type of project. Over the course of several years and several technology acquisitions, I was able to develop and fine tune a project life cycle that addresses this need.

Figure I-2 represents the project life cycle for managing a technology acquisition project.

Figure I-2: Technology acquisition project life cycle

The process begins with the *Initiation* phase. All projects are initiated. Sometimes this process takes a few minutes and other times it takes months. The important thing to determine is what the business need is. You can then create a project or projects to implement the solution(s) selected to address that business need. The Initiation phase is described in greater detail in Chapter 1.

Once the project has been properly initiated, the *Planning* phase begins. During this phase, the following tasks take place:

- Project plans are developed

- A project team is developed

- Requirements are defined and prioritized

- A solution is defined

- Vendors are identified and contacted.

The Planning phase is described in greater detail in Chapter 2.

All activities involved in researching the vendors and their technologies are included in the *Research* phase. There are several methods that can be used to research vendors. Chapter 3 provides a detailed description of several research methods and discusses when it is appropriate to use each method.

Once you have completed the research, it is time to evaluate the results and select a vendor. These activities take place during the *Evaluation* phase. Chapter 4 provides a detailed description of the techniques used to evaluate and select a vendor.

The activities involved in negotiating a contract with the selected vendor are part of the *Negotiation* phase. Chapter 5 discusses the negotiation strategy, tactics, planning, and documentation.

After the technology is selected and the contracts are signed, the *Implementation* phase begins. Chapter 6 discusses the processes for developing, testing, and deploying vendor solutions.

The final phase of the technology acquisition is the *Operations* phase. This process extends throughout the life of the product. Chapter 7 defines the details surrounding the continuing support process.

Many case studies are inserted throughout the book. These examples are derived from real-life situations. A fictional name (Jack Smith) and company (XYZ Corporation) have been substituted in order to honor the confidentiality agreements that always exist in this type of project.

The People

Although few will argue the importance of process, the people involved in the technology acquisition are equally, if not more, important. People dynamics can make or break a technology acquisition. One of the most important objectives of the technology acquisition process is to objectify a subjective decision about which vendor and solution is best for your situation. The processes included in the project life cycle described in this book are designed to accomplish this by breaking a large subjective decision down into many small subjective and objective decisions. This will objectify the overall decision as much as possible. With that said, people will still have a significant influence on the final decision. At times, they will even override it. It is unrealistic to think that a process or a formula can provide the answer, with 100 percent accuracy, to such a complex question of which vendor and technology are best for your current situation. What a process can do is help people make a more educated decision and understand what is being decided. A significant portion of this book is dedicated to the people involved in the technology acquisition project and the roles and functions that they provide.

Many groups of people are involved in a technology acquisition. Table I-1 lists the primary groups involved in this type of project.

Table I-1: Technology Acquisition Teams and Members

Group	Organization	Involvement
Project sponsor	Customer or IT	Medium
Project stakeholders	Customer, IT, and vendor	Low
Project manager	Customer or IT	High
Project team	Customer and IT	Medium
Vendor sales team	Vendor sales	High
Negotiation team	Customer, IT, and legal	Medium
Internal Implementation team	Customer and IT	High
Vendor Implementation team	Vendor consulting	High
Internal support team	IT	Medium
Vendor support team	Vendor support	Medium
End User	Customer	High

The members and groups listed in Table I-1 are discussed in greater detail in their appropriate chapters throughout the book. After reading these chapters, you should have a good understanding of who they are and what their roles, challenges, opportunities, and motives are.

The Tools

This book also provides a set of templates and sample documents that can be used in a technology acquisition project. Your company may already have standard templates for some of these documents. If not, these samples will help you create your own templates and documents for your first technology acquisition project.

The sample documents were used in actual technology acquisition projects, but the data has been modified in order to honor the confidentiality agreements that are essential in this type of project. The samples shown are the best examples and formats used in a number of projects; all content has been modified to simulate a fictitious technology acquisition project.

1

Initiation

How does a project start? Do all projects start the same way? Are all projects justified? These are some of the questions that are discussed in Chapter 1. The Initiation phase includes all activities that define a new project.

＊ The objective of the Initiation phase is to clearly define the business need,✻ define and develop a solution to address the need, create a business case to justify the solution, and begin to define the initiative in a project charter.

Some argue that this phase is the most important of all the phases in the project life cycle. The argument contends that you can select the best technologies and employ the best project management practices, but if you aren't addressing the right business need, you may be wasting your time. Ensuring that the business need is clearly defined and that there is a sufficient business case for the intended solution will set your project in the right direction.

Chapter 1 discusses the process for the Initiation phase. Major activities include defining a business need and chartering a project. Also discussed are the project sponsor and the project stakeholders and the roles they play in the technology acquisition.

THE INITIATION PROCESS

The Initiation process consists of two subprocesses: the business need and the project charter (Figure 1-1).

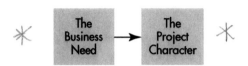

Figure 1-1: Initiation subprocesses

"The Business Need" section of this chapter discusses how projects begin. Generally, a project is initiated with a problem or an opportunity. Examples of both are provided. Developing a business need document that will help communicate the business need is discussed as well.

The final subprocess of the Initiation process is the project charter. "The Project Charter" section defines what a project charter is, why it is important, and what it includes.

The Business Need

Projects are usually created as a result of a business defining one or more business needs. A definition of a business need follows:

> **Business Need:** A defined change to the current state of a business that will benefit the business in some way.

Business needs can be identified either as an opportunity for improvement or as a problem that must be resolved. Table 1-1 provides a list of examples for each type of business need.

Business needs are usually identified by people who work within a business organization. The key to defining a good business need is that it does not try to identify a solution. It only states what business need should be addressed.

Clearly defining the business need is often one of the most significant tasks in a successful project. Even the best technology and project management practices will not ensure success if the project addresses the wrong business need. Many times, people jump to a technology solution and fail to clearly understand what the business really needs.

Table 1-1: Business Need Examples

Opportunities for Improvement	Problems to Be Resolved
Reduction in support costs	Increase in employee turnover
Increased revenue opportunity	Loss of market share
Reduction in labor costs	Poor customer service ratings
Improved customer service	Shipping product to the wrong address
Improved quality	Lack of product inventory information in Sales department
Improved decision support	Current technology is outdated

It is important to verify the business need by collecting all of the facts supporting the need. This can be accomplished in several ways. You can define the current process and collect all of the measurements for each step of the process. You can interview or survey employees or customers. Or, you can acquire external data that supports the business need. The key is to collect as much data as you possibly can in a reasonable amount of time. Most likely, you will find facts that support the business need.

Just as important as defining the facts is defining the assumptions. Therefore, you need to determine what assumptions are being made in acknowledging the business need. Having a clear understanding of the assumptions will help you understand the risks of pursuing the wrong business need. (See the Case Study: Addressing the Wrong Business Need.)

Case Study

ADDRESSING THE WRONG BUSINESS NEED

Jack Smith of XYZ Corporation, a project manager for a call center that supported the company's personal computers, was assigned a project to address a business need that was affecting all technicians in the call center. The problem was that the knowledgebase that the technicians used to find solutions to common problems was too slow and extended the average call times.

Jack set out to solve the problem by developing a more streamlined graphic user interface (GUI) to the knowledgebase. Jack contacted the company who

(continued)

Case Study (continued)

sold XYZ the knowledgebase and contracted a few consultants to help develop the new and improved GUI. The design, development, and testing phases were managed effectively, and the new GUI was ready on time and under budget. Jack began getting a lot of recognition for his ability to get things done.

The new GUI was deployed to one team of technicians to test it and see if it improved performance. After weeks of piloting the new GUI, the performance numbers hadn't changed at all. Jack was amazed and couldn't understand how this could be. The new user interface was much easier to use to navigate through the knowledgebase. Jack decided to call a meeting with the technicians involved in the pilot to see if they had any ideas as to why this new and improved GUI was not improving performance.

Jack couldn't believe what he heard from the technicians. Apparently, the reason the knowledgebase was slow was not due to the user interface at all. The problem was that the data in the knowledgebase was structured in a way that required the technicians to drill down through many levels of categorization before they could get to a solution. What they really needed was for someone to restructure the data in the knowledgebase.

The bottom line was that Jack hadn't bothered to validate the business need and ensure that he was addressing the right problem. The project was considered a failure and a waste of time and money, which could have been used for something that would improve the business.

LESSON LEARNED
Always research and validate the business need to understand any assumptions that are made before defining a solution.

Once you have analyzed the business need and are confident that you have identified all of the facts and assumptions, you need to document them in a business need document. The business need document will help to clearly communicate the business need to others who will be involved in addressing the need later in the process.

In some organizations, a business need is used as input to the strategic planning process. Management evaluates a number of business needs and decides whether to pursue a solution for each need. In other organizations, a manager with authority over the organization with the business need decides whether or not to pursue a solution for the specific need.

At the time the decision is made to pursue a solution to the business need, a project sponsor is assigned to own the initiative. The project sponsor is held accountable for addressing the business need by his or her management. See the following business need template and sample for more details.

Template

BUSINESS NEED

CONTEXT
Describes the current state of the business and lays out the context surrounding the business needs that this project needs to address.

BUSINESS NEED
Describes the business problem or opportunity that the project needs to address. Be careful not to define solutions in this section. It is also a good idea to be as specific as possible, leaving no room for misinterpretation.

SUPPORTING FACTS
Contains the facts that support the business needs. This section should provide quantitative measurements that support each business need. You should also specify the source of the data used in the measurements.

ASSUMPTIONS
Lists all of the assumptions (estimates or statements that lack supporting data) so that the decision makers know what decision they are making.

APPROVALS
Includes approvals for each business sponsor or stakeholder that has the business need.

Chartering the Project

The role of the project charter is to clearly define *what* the project is. It is a good idea to separate the definition of *what* the project is from the definitions of the *how*, *when*, *where*, and *who* of the project, which are typically addressed in the project plan. This approach is recommended for two reasons. First, a different audience is typically responsible for defining *what* the project is. The business sponsors and

SAMPLE BUSINESS NEED

1. Context

XYZ supports its customers via a number of delivery options: traditional phone support, Internet and online services, letters and faxes, automated attendant/troubleshooting systems, FaxBack systems, and mail-in service. Customer Support is segmented in the following manner:

- General Technical Support (supporting individuals, families, enthusiasts, small businesses, and education customers)
- Major Accounts Support (for large, corporate customers and government agencies)
- International Support (customers owning XYZ calculators in international regions not covered by XYZ international sites)
- Customer Service (nontechnical support, such as order status, cancellations, refunds, etc.)

Each of these groups has its own forecast and requires workforce scheduling.

XYZ uses the services of several outsource call centers to enhance its availability to its customers. We currently provide a monthly and interval forecast to each outsource center, which in turn does its own scheduling. The strategic plan calls for a ramp-down in the percentage of calls XYZ outsources. Outsource companies currently handle (30%) of XYZ's overall support volume. Our internal support is currently spread across 12 U.S. sites, and we will add four more by year's end.

XYZ routes its calls in the following manner: Customers call 800 numbers and choose options from a conversant. Using XXX Intelligent Call Router, calls are distributed to the center, which real-time calculation suggests has the shortest answer time. Some calls are still routed using percent allocation from an AAA platform.

2. Business Need

- Need the ability to segment our support call volumes to facilitate both internal productivity and the optimal customer experience. This requires extensive modeling (given the fact that we're a multisite environment layered with several customer segments and business segments).
- Need the ability to create optimum workforce schedules based on projected call volumes.
- Need to implement some "down-the-wire" support strategies to aid productivity and call resolution rates.

3. Supporting Facts

XYZ is currently handling approximately 16,000 calls per day, distributed as follows in each of the following segments: General: (10,000 total, and 7,000 internal versus 3,000 external, AHT = 15 min.) Major Accounts: (1,500 internal, AHT= 11 min.) International: (500 internal, AHT = 12 min.) Customer Service: (4,000 internal, AHT = 3 min.)

4. Assumptions
We expect volume to increase by (35%) in the next 12 months.

5. Approvals

stakeholders define the project charter, whereas the project manager and project team develop the project plan. Second, the project charter requires different approvals and shouldn't change very much during the project. On the other hand, the project plan and the defined solution could change several times throughout the project. Having a clearly defined project charter with the appropriate approvals provides the project team members with a clear understanding of the business need they are to address. See the following project charter template and sample for more details.

Template

PROJECT CHARTER

EXECUTIVE SUMMARY
Provides a summary of each section in this document at a very high level. This section is typically created after the rest of the document is complete. The goal when creating an executive summary is to be concise and limit it to one page.

BUSINESS NEED
Describes the current state of the business and lays out the context surrounding the business needs that this project needs to address. This section is typically copied from the Business Need document.

PROJECT OBJECTIVE
Describes the proposed solution that addresses the business needs. In this type of project, this section should state that a certain type of technology will be acquired to address the business need.

(continued)

Template (continued)

IMPACT ASSESSMENT
Defines the impact that the proposed solution will have on the business. This should be divided into two groups. The first group lists the benefits that will be realized by successfully completing the proposed project. The second group lists the consequences of not completing the proposed project. In other words, it describes what will happen if no action is taken to address the business need.

MEASUREMENT OF SUCCESS
Describes how you will measure success. The more specific you can be the better. These success measurements are quantifiable and leave no question of whether you are successful in achieving them. It is also beneficial to list the goal first and then follow it with the minimum measurement for the project to be considered successful.

SCOPE
Defines what the project is and what it is not. This is your opportunity to clearly state where the project starts and where it ends. Some people call this "drawing a box around the initiative." The benefit of defining the scope in great detail at the outset is that it ensures that everyone involved has the same perception of what business needs the project will address and what end result the project will produce.

RISKS
Lists the risks involved in pursuing the project as well as the risks to the success of the project. You should also list the probability (as a percentage) and categorize the impact (high/medium/low). At a minimum, it is recommended that you clearly define the impact of the risks that are either high probability or high in impact.

TIME CONSTRAINTS
Defines time constraints, if any, imposed on the project. For example, your company may have a policy or unwritten rule that nothing can be implemented during the holiday season. Another example would be a dependency on the time frame of another project that must be completed before this project can be implemented.

STAKEHOLDER AND SPONSOR APPROVAL
Includes approvals for each stakeholder impacted by the project and each business sponsor who will be funding the project.

SAMPLE PROJECT CHARTER

1. Executive Summary
XYZ Corporation currently creates workforce schedules manually. There is an opportunity to acquire technology that will assist in creating optimal workforce schedules using projected call volumes based on historical data.

2. Business Need
- Need the ability to segment our support call volumes to facilitate both internal productivity and the optimal customer experience. This requires extensive modeling (given the fact that we're a multisite environment layered with several customer segments and business segments).
- Need the ability to create optimum workforce schedules based on projected call volumes.
- Need to implement some "down-the-wire" support strategies to aid productivity and call resolution rates.

3. Project Objectives
Apply technology to enable development of optimal workforce schedules based on projected call volumes.

4. Impact Assessment
Improved workforce schedule efficiency.

5. Measures of Success
This project will be considered successful if the number of calls supported by the existing internal workforce increases by more than 10 percent.

6. Scope
This project addresses workforce scheduling for all internal and external call centers at XYZ.

7. Risks
- Historical data inaccuracy will have a negative impact on projecting future data volumes.
- Employee satisfaction could suffer based on schedule changes resulting from this initiative.

8. Time Constraints
This project must be completed prior to the next holiday season to minimize the number of calls that will need to be outsourced due to the increased volume.

9. Project Stakeholder and Sponsor Approvals

When preparing to charter a project, you should spend some time ensuring that you have identified all of the project stakeholders and have received a commitment from them to participate in the project chartering sessions. It may be necessary to get business executive sponsorship buy-in before approaching project stakeholders. This will ensure that the appropriate level of priority and commitment will be given to the chartering effort.

Once you have identified all project stakeholders to attend the project chartering sessions, you need to begin planning the chartering sessions and scheduling the times and locations. You should also plan a meeting with the project stakeholders to educate them on the business need, the project charter template, and the charter session format. Taking the time to preview these items with them in advance will ensure that you make the best use of their time during the chartering sessions.

It is also a good idea to create a draft of the project charter prior to the chartering session. Starting from scratch will take longer and will waste the project stakeholders' time. If you present a draft to the project stakeholders, you will be able to focus them on the task at hand and give them an idea of what each section of the project charter should contain.

Chartering sessions should begin with introductions, a review of the agenda, and a brief introduction to the business need. Once this is complete, take the time to go through the document format describing each section. This will provide an understanding of what will be covered during the session so that there is less confusion. For example, attendees may try to define scope when discussing the business needs. If they know that scope will be discussed later in the charter session, they will be more focused on the objectives of each section.

When facilitating a chartering session, you should pay attention to the agenda and know when a discussion is getting too far off track. It may be necessary to keep a list of action items and items to be addressed at a different time (e.g., parking lot items). This allows the facilitator to capture the topic and table it for a later discussion.

Another decision you should make is whether to pass out printed versions of the draft project charter for the meeting or to bring a laptop and present the charter to the entire group at once. Many facilitators have found it beneficial to use projection systems and edit the document as a team during the meeting. This approach tends to keep the stakeholders from reading ahead and keeps them focused on participating in the group discussion. If you take this approach, make sure you have someone other than the facilitator make the changes on the laptop. This allows the facilitator to keep the pace of the meeting moving forward while the scribe is busy editing the document.

Chartering sessions can be very valuable in establishing alignment in the definition of what the project is supposed to accomplish. In most cases, each stakeholder has a slightly different idea of what the project is prior to the chartering effort. Discussing the project details as a group will help you achieve consensus among the project stakeholders.

You may need to schedule several project chartering sessions to review updates to the charter from the first session. It is important that each project stakeholder sign the final project charter. Although some will say the signatures aren't important, you will find that people will pay more attention to the details if they know that they have to sign their names in approval of the content in the charter. Additionally, the project sponsor will want to be sure that all project stakeholders approve of the charter before the sponsor approves it and takes it to the executive sponsors.

The executive sponsors and project sponsor will be better able to prioritize and schedule a project if they have a clear understanding of what the project is. The project charter will provide this understanding so that they can determine the best time to begin the project. The project sponsor will also have a better understanding of which project manager is best suited to manage the project.

Once you have an approved project charter in hand, you should start the project change management process. If your company has a formal change management process, leverage it and begin tracking changes to the project, including changes to the project charter, using the process. If your company doesn't have a formal change management process, create one for the project. This process should include steps for identifying, quantifying impacts for, communicating, and approving each change. There should also be a set of thresholds that determine what level of approval is required. For example, you may decide that any change that impacts the schedule by two weeks or the budget by $100,000 requires project sponsor approval.

Communicate the project charter throughout your organization so that management from all parts of the company has a clear understanding of what the project is. At a minimum, all project team members and all project stakeholder organizations should receive a copy of the approved project charter. This allows them to prepare for the end result of the project or to bring up changes, issues, and risks to the project team. The following case study reinforces the value of communicating the approved project charter.

Case Study

COMMUNICATING THE PROJECT CHARTER

Jack Smith was managing a technology acquisition project to buy 100 licenses of a technology for a small department. After communicating the project charter to the enterprise, another department said that it would need 1,000 licenses of this technology in the future. Jack made sure to let the vendor know during negotiations that XYZ Corporation was looking for a technology partner for the long term, and that there was another department within the company that would potentially be using this technology in the future. The prospect of 1,000 additional licenses was enough leverage to negotiate a more favorable deal in the short term. XYZ Corporation approached the vendor as if it were locking in a price for 1,100 licenses instead of 100 licenses. You can imagine how this information improved the pricing.

If Jack hadn't taken the time to communicate the project charter throughout the company, he might not have known about the other department's need for the same technology. He was also able to include representatives from the other department on the project team to ensure that they had a voice in the decision of which vendor to pursue a relationship with. They were also able to become educated about the vendor and the technology, which would help them implement it in their department when the time came.

LESSON LEARNED
Always communicate the project charter within your organization.

The following checklist is provided as an aid to help you complete the tasks necessary for the Initiation process.

INITIATION PROCESS CHECKLIST

❑ *The business need has been clearly articulated in writing.*

❑ *All assumptions for the business need are documented.*

❑ *The project has been chartered and clearly defines the effort.*

❑ *The project charter has been approved by all stakeholders and the project sponsor.*

❑ *The project charter has been communicated to all relevant organizations.*

✳ THE PROJECT SPONSOR ✳

The project sponsor is ultimately responsible for the success or failure of a technology acquisition. Executive management and project stakeholders look to the project sponsor to ensure that the objectives of the technology acquisition are achieved as stated in the project charter. The role of the project sponsor in a technology acquisition is to provide leadership to the project and act as the champion of the cause within the organization.

A project sponsor is typically a manager, director, or vice president, depending on the scope of the initiative. Typically, this person is a member of the organization most impacted by the project. In the case where several organizations are impacted by the project, the project sponsor may be a member of the Information Technology (IT) organization. It is important that a project sponsor have authority, clout, and respect within the organization.

To ensure that the technology acquisition is successful, the project sponsor's responsibilities include providing leadership, championing the cause, decision making, and accountability.

Leadership versus Management

The differences between leadership and management are outlined in the following definitions.

Leadership: Providing vision, direction, and guidance to an organization or initiative.

Management: Overseeing the planning, execution, and control of an organization or initiative.

The project sponsor is primarily responsible for providing leadership to the technology acquisition, whereas the project manager is responsible for providing management to the technology acquisition.

The project sponsor assigns the project manager to the technology acquisition. The project sponsor also provides leadership to the project manager and provides support throughout the project. Inevitably, the project manager will run into several obstacles throughout the project that he will be unable to overcome. It is the project sponsor's role to remove these obstacles, enabling the project manager to keep the project on schedule, within budget, and be able meet the requirements stated in the project charter.

Champion of the Cause

The project sponsor is also responsible for playing the role of champion of the cause for the technology acquisition. It is the job of the project sponsor to communicate the vision of the project to executive management, stakeholders, and vendors. The project sponsor will need to rally support and ensure buy-in of the goals and objectives of the project. It is important that the project sponsor meet with each of the stakeholder organizations to make sure they understand the vision and agree with the priorities of the project.

Decision Making

The primary goal of the technology acquisition process is to objectify what is ultimately a subjective decision. The project sponsor makes the final subjective decision because he is responsible for the overall project. In order to ensure that he makes the best possible decision for a company, the project sponsor initiates a process, such as the technology acquisition process described in this book, to help him objectify the decision as much as possible. The project team researches and evaluates the details of each vendor and its technology in order to make a recommendation, which may or may not be accepted by the project sponsor. As long as the project sponsor understands the implications of the decision he is making, not accepting the recommendation from the project team is justified. An extensive technology acquisition provides the team with as much information as reasonably possible about the decision he makes.

The project manager may also elect to escalate key issues to the project sponsor, such as scope and priority issues. The project sponsor needs to weigh the pros and cons and make appropriate decisions. Rarely will the project sponsor escalate a decision to executive management because it is understood that he is the one being held accountable for the outcome of the project.

Accountability

Being accountable is a double-edged sword. In order to be a good leader, you need to prove that you can be given a goal to accomplish and then deliver on that promise. A reliable leader who can accomplish objectives critical to the mission of the company will surely rise up in the ranks quickly. On the other hand, there is also a downside to being accountable. You may be unsuccessful due to challenges outside of your control. Excuses will not do you any good with executive management. Companies cannot afford to make many mistakes in a competitive environment. If a project sponsor is labeled as unreliable, he will not be given responsibility for key projects, which significantly limits his career growth.

✳ THE PROJECT MANAGER ✳

The profession of project management is becoming increasingly important as companies continue to outsource, multisource, and contract out work that was previously handled in-house. The role of the project manager is to gather and manage the resources required to complete project objectives. A project manager is like a symphony conductor. A conductor needs to know how each of the instruments should sound and how each can be integrated with the other instruments to create a desired sound. Likewise, a project manager needs to understand what skill sets are required in project team resources and how they can be integrated to accomplish the objective of the project.

Project managers typically come from a business or technical analyst role. This can be both an advantage and a disadvantage. The advantage is that they can use their subject matter expertise to improve their ability to plan, execute, and control project activities related to that subject area. One disadvantage is that they sometimes assume that they know the requirements of the subject area and fail to allow that subject area to define its own requirements. This can cause the subject area to not support the project, potentially delaying or ending the project altogether. Another disadvantage of project managers having subject matter expertise is that they sometimes resist embracing project management fundamentals. Skipping the fundamentals, such as clearly defining requirements, can doom a project to failure. When project managers lack subject matter expertise, they are forced to rely on the fundamentals and to leverage the expertise already in the subject matter area.

Objectivity

Usually, it is easier to manage a technology acquisition from an objective viewpoint. This requires a shift in mind-set from influencing to facilitating. Your focus becomes managing the project team through a decision-making process and not trying to influence the decision yourself.

There may come a time during the process when your project team members have different viewpoints. These team members will try to influence other team members to see things their way. A project manager who tries to influence team members can be disastrous if he gives one vendor an advantage over another. One of the project manager's primary goals in facilitating the technology acquisition process is to create a fair and competitive environment for all vendors participating in the process. For this reason, it is easier to be objective if you are not one of the decision makers.

Maneuvering a Project through an Organization

Maneuvering a project through an organization can be very challenging. There are usually several factors impacting your ability to meet timelines and stay within budget. Project managers with organizational savvy are able to avoid and overcome these factors and keep a project on track. Most project managers with experience managing technology acquisitions will tell you that it is often easier to negotiate with vendors than it is to negotiate within your own organization. I have found this to be true in my experience as well. Many internal and external obstacles and influences can emerge during a technology acquisition.

Internal obstacles and influences can come from many different areas within your organization. The following list examines a few of these areas:

- *Stakeholder motives:* When stakeholder motives are not in alignment with the objectives of the project, there is a good chance that your project will experience some setbacks along the way. For example, if a key stakeholder is set on one solution, and your project is scoped to pursue another, the stakeholder may try to put a stop to your project. As a project manager, your job is to keep this from happening in the first place by ensuring that all stakeholders have had their chance to provide input in the decision process during the Initiation phase. There will be times when you cannot plan ahead, such as when a change of leadership within a stakeholder organization occurs. The best thing to do when faced with a resistant stakeholder is to provide the organization with the project charter and help the stakeholder understand the process that needs to be followed in order to get executive management buy-in on any changes to the scope of the project charter. If your organization doesn't already have a change management process, you should plan for one at the beginning of the project in order to deal with these unexpected changes when they arise.

- *Budget cuts:* Most of the time, public companies almost always tighten their purse strings in the fourth quarter of their fiscal year. Executive management begins to get a better idea of whether or not the company will meet its earnings projections. Expense cutting measures are implemented to delay or eliminate as many expenses as possible. If you are managing a technology acquisition during this time, you will be expected to contribute by minimizing your expenses as well. Typical expenses that will be scrutinized are travel, training, and salaries. You can avoid these challenges by planning your expenses around the fourth quarter.

- *Executive management:* Executive management decisions are the hardest obstacle to overcome. When executive management decides to change, delay, or end a project, there is little you can do to change that decision. What you can do is be prepared at all times with a solid business case and strong support from the stakeholder organizations. When a number of projects are under consideration for cancellation, it is sometimes the project whose stakeholders scream the loudest that survives.

- *Change:* Any type of change that impacts the technology acquisition needs to be managed by the project manager. Try to get ahead of the game by identifying potential changes as risks to the success of the project. Once risks are identified, you can define appropriate risk responses (e.g., acceptance, avoidance, elimination, or reduction).

External obstacles and influences can come from the market, vendors, or your competition. The following list examines a few:

- *Vendor situations:* Vendor situations, such as lawsuits or bankruptcy filings, can impact your technology acquisition process. Be sure to research your vendors thoroughly to understand their financial status and customer satisfaction ratings (see Chapter 3 for an understanding of the Research process). Other than that, all you can do is make sure you always have more than one vendor in the process until the contracts are signed.

- *New technology:* Changes in technology can cause your management team to reevaluate the decisions that were made regarding which solution to pursue in addressing the business need. It is difficult to see into the future in order to avoid this situation. All you can do is make sure you are evaluating vendors with a reputation for technology leadership. Most technology-driven vendors will tell you where their technology and the industry's technology are headed if you have signed a confidentiality agreement.

- *Competitor solutions:* The competition may implement a new program that addresses the same business need more effectively or efficiently than the proposed solution. This can sometimes cause your executive management team to revisit the solution that you are currently pursuing.

- *Economic conditions:* Changes in the economy can have an impact on your technology acquisition. For example, if the economy is experiencing a slowdown, your company may put your project on hold as a result.

- *Vendor market conditions:* Changes in the vendor's market can create an obstacle for your project. For example, if the vendors are growing too fast due to demand, they may not be able to take on additional business within your time frames. The only way you can address this is to have a good feel for the market conditions and the direction of the market when deciding on which solution to pursue in addressing the business need.

Integrity

When managing a technology acquisition, you will have vendors doing their best to influence you. This is usually accomplished fairly with good salesmanship. But, there will eventually come a time when a vendor tries to influence you through unfair, unlawful, or unethical methods. These can come in the form of future job offers, cash, gifts (for example, cars), blackmail, or threats. This may sound a bit hard to believe but it does happen. My advice is to be ready for it and make sure that you handle it quickly and severely. Vendors who use unacceptable methods during the sales process will probably use unacceptable methods during the duration of your relationship with them. If they cross the line, make them aware that their behavior is not acceptable, and that you will have your management contact their management to address your concerns. Immediately contact the project sponsor and make him aware of the situation. This then becomes the company's issue and not yours personally.

As a project manager, one of your greatest assets is your integrity. If you gain a reputation for being trustworthy and reliable, you will go far in the profession. Don't allow a short-term gain to put your long-term career at risk.

✳THE PROJECT STAKEHOLDERS✳

A stakeholder is an individual or organization impacted by the success or failure of the technology acquisition project. The impact can be positive or negative. The following illustrates what a list of stakeholders might look like for a project to acquire a Point of Sale (POS) system for a retail store:

- Retail customers

- Retail employees

- Retail store managers

- Retail operations organization

- IT retail systems organization

- IT production support organizations

- Accounting organization

- Merchandise organization

- Supply chain organization

Stakeholder support is critical in a technology acquisition. This is why some organizations select project sponsors from the stakeholder organization that is most impacted by the new technology. Regardless of where the project sponsor comes from, he needs to balance the needs of all stakeholder organizations. Stakeholders may not have the final say in the decision of which vendor to select, but they will have a say in whether the technology ever sees daylight in their organization and whether there is a commitment to make it a success.

Stakeholder Motives

Project sponsors and project managers need to understand who the stakeholders are and their motives (Table 1-2) in order to work with them successfully.

Stakeholders have commonly acknowledged motives that everyone is aware of. There are also unacknowledged motives (hidden agendas) of which few are aware. It is critical that the project sponsor and project manager identify and understand the hidden agendas to ensure that the project is undertaken for the right reasons. This is not always as easy as it sounds. One way to identify hidden agendas is to put yourself in the stakeholders' shoes and try to understand how they might benefit from the project and how the project might be a threat to them. Another way is to meet with them individually and ask about alternative motives. If asked the right way, they might share their hidden agendas with you in confidence.

Table 1-2: Sample List of Stakeholder Motives

Stakeholders	Motives
Retail customers	Purchase quality products
	Fast service
Retail store employees	Sell product
	Satisfy customers
Retail store managers	Satisfy customers
	Increase profitability
	Manage store operations
Retail operations organization	Improve efficiency of store operations
IT retail systems organization	Provide information systems that support the goals of the retail organizations
IT production support organizations	Support the operation of the information systems
Accounting organization	Track and manage retail store finances
	Payroll
Merchandise organization	Plan and coordinate merchandise product selections for all retail stores
Supply chain organization	Distribute product to the retail stores at the right time
	Improve efficiency of supply chain operations

Organizational Influence

It is also a good idea to think about the influence of each of the stakeholder organizations. If one stakeholder organization has significant influence over the other stakeholders, getting its buy-in often ensures buy-in from the other stakeholders as well.

A stakeholder with significant influence on executive management may also help you justify and sell the project within an organization. This can provide the credibility you need to get approval to proceed with the technology acquisition project.

Defining Priorities

An important role that the stakeholders play is to define the priorities for the project. It makes sense that the organizations that are impacted by the technology define which requirements are the highest in priority.

If a project stakeholder has not been involved in setting priorities, it will not be able to provide you with the information that will enable you to select a solution that meets its needs.

Getting Consensus

Getting consensus is important to a point. You want to achieve buy-in from the key stakeholders to ensure proper support. On the other hand, there will be times when stakeholders do not agree with the initiative but the project proceeds anyway. If the benefits to one stakeholder outweigh the drawbacks to another stakeholder, a business decision may be made to pursue the solution and live with the drawbacks. The stakeholder that will realize the drawbacks to the solution will likely not support the project, and there will be times when there is nothing you can do about that.

The project sponsor creates consensus between stakeholders using two approaches. The first is to meet with each stakeholder individually and give that person the opportunity to clearly understand the business need and proposed solution and provide feedback. The second is to ask each stakeholder to allocate a Subject Matter Expert (SME) to the technology acquisition project team to represent the organization's business requirements throughout the process. People are more likely to embrace a new technology if they are included in the process of acquiring it.

2

Planning

In the Planning phase of the technology acquisition, you determine the answers to the following questions:

- How will you research, evaluate, and negotiate with vendors?

- How will you implement and operate your solution?

- Who will be responsible for each activity?

- When must these activities occur in order to meet the project time objectives?

- Where will the activities take place?

In this chapter, the process of planning the acquisition, defining requirements, prioritizing requirements, defining the solution, and identifying and contacting vendors are discussed.

Additionally, the role of a technology acquisition project manager is defined, if it hasn't already been assigned during the Initiation phase. Assigning the right project manager can make or break a technology acquisition. You will learn what qualities make a project manager successful.

The different roles of the project team are also discussed in detail in this chapter. Ensuring that the right combination of people exist on the team is critical to selecting the right technology for your business.

THE PLANNING PROCESS

The Planning process consists of five subprocesses: project planning, requirements definition, prioritization, the solution, and identifying and contacting vendors (Figure 2-1).

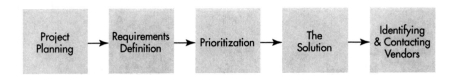

Figure 2-1: Planning subprocesses

Project planning is the process of identifying all of the work to be done and organizing it into a manageable plan, which includes developing a project plan and a project schedule.

It is very important that you know what the stakeholder organizations need before you start researching and evaluating vendors and their technologies. This includes defining the functionality, technology, strategic partnership, and cost requirements.

The output of the requirements definition is a list of requirements that may include everything from "nice to have" to "must have" business requirements (also called showstoppers). The "Prioritization" section of this chapter provides a tool to help you define this list. It helps you understand what is important in evaluating vendors and enables you to objectify the decision-making process.

The "Defining the Solution" section discusses identifying solutions, analyzing solutions, selecting a solution, making the buy versus build decision, and developing a business case to justify the selected solution. By the end of this subprocess, you should have a detailed understanding of *how* the project will address the business need.

How do you determine which vendors to include in your technology acquisition process? The last section in this chapter, "Identifying and Contacting Vendors" describes several methods of identifying vendors for your acquisition. This section also discusses how to make the initial contact through the use of a letter of intent (LOI) and nondisclosure agreement (NDA).

The Project Plan

The purpose of the project plan is to provide a tool for the project manager to visualize, track, manage, and understand all activities required to successfully complete a project. It is also a tool used to communicate the plan to the project team, project sponsor, stakeholders, and executive management. It is important to distinguish the difference between a project plan and a project schedule.

A project plan should include all planning activities that are required to execute and control the project including plans to manage the change, risk, issues, products, quality, communication, releases, human resources, and costs (see the following project plan template and sample).

Because these additional planning activities are covered in several other project management books, they will not be covered in great detail. See the Resources appendix at the end of this book for additional information on these planning activities.

Template
_____

PROJECT PLAN

PROJECT MANAGEMENT PLAN
Defines the methodology that will be used and the approach to managing the activities and tasks required to complete the project.

RISK MANAGEMENT PLAN
Describes the processes and tools that will be used to track and manage the identification, planning, assessment, quantification, response, and mitigation strategy for each risk in the project.

ISSUE MANAGEMENT PLAN
Describes the processes and tools that will be used to track and manage the prioritization, delegation, status, and resolution of project issues.

(continued)

Template (continued)

CHANGE MANAGEMENT PLAN
Describes the processes and tools that will be used to track and manage the changes to the project or product of the project and impact assessments and approvals for each change.

QUALITY MANAGEMENT PLAN
Describes the processes and tools that will be used to track and manage quality throughout the project. This plan may include quality assurance and quality control.

PRODUCT MANAGEMENT PLAN
Describes the processes and tools that will be used to track and manage product requirements, definition, and design specifications.

RELEASE MANAGEMENT PLAN
Describes the processes and tools that will be used to track and manage multiple product versions that will be implemented as a suite of products in a release.

HUMAN RESOURCE MANAGEMENT PLAN
Describes the processes and tools that will be used to track and manage human resources for the duration of the project. It is also common to list the roles, requirements, and team members in this section of the Project Plan.

COST MANAGEMENT PLAN
Describes the processes and tools that will be used to track and manage costs and variances between budgeted, planned, and actual costs for the project.

The Project Schedule

A project schedule typically includes a list of activities and tasks. Tasks represent the actual work to be completed. It is at the task level that work is assigned to resources. Once a list of activities and associated tasks are defined, you can add more detail to each task, such as duration, dependencies, resources, costs, and start and finish dates. You should also define the key milestones for the project. It is recommended that you invest in project scheduling software if your company does not already provide this software. Project scheduling software allows you to look at activities in

SAMPLE Project Plan

1. Project Management Plan

The following diagram represents the project life cycle that will be used to manage this project:

The detailed project schedule is attached to the appendix of this document.

2. Risk Management Plan

Risks will be managed using the department's program database and reviewed in the weekly Project Plan Review (PPR) meetings.

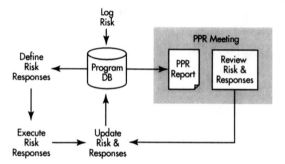

3. Issue Management Plan

Issues will be managed using the department's program database and reviewed in the weekly Project Plan Review (PPR) meetings.

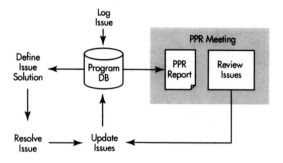

(continued)

SAMPLE Project Plan (*continued*)

4. Change Management Plan

Changes will be managed using the department's program database and reviewed in the weekly Project Plan Review (PPR) meetings.

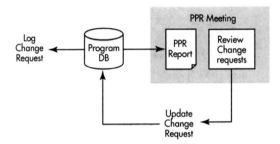

5. Quality Management Plan

The Quality Control team will test the solution using the department standard testing procedures prior to implementation.

6. Product Management Plan

Modifications to the vendor's product will be tracked and managed in the program database. There will be a weekly product change review meeting with the vendor.

7. Release Management Plan

There is no need for an extended release management plan for this project.

8. Human Resource Management Plan

The following diagram represents the project organization for this project.

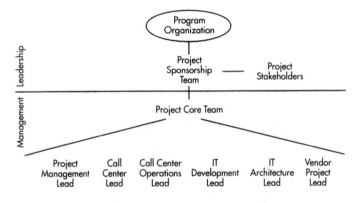

The roles and responsibilities of each team member are as follows.

Project Sponsorship Team:

- Apply leadership to the project
- Support the project manager and the project core team leads
- Provide project decision making and issue resolution when appropriate
- Escalate issues to program management and executive management when appropriate
- Provide resources to the project core team
- Communicate issues to the project core team
- Communicate project status to representative departments

Project Management Lead:

- Apply project management practices to plan, execute, and control all project activities
- Own and manage the project plans and schedules
- Monitor and ensure compliance to program processes
- Escalate key risks, issues, and project changes to project sponsorship and program management
- Communicate project status to project sponsorship and program management
- Assign and manage project core team lead roles (including vendor project managers)

Call Center Lead:

- Primary liaison between the call centers and the project team
- Define call center priorities
- Manage and coordinate call center requirements definition
- Communicate project status to the call centers
- Manage and coordinate all call center project activities
- Provide regular updates to project manager on all activities

Call Center Operations Lead:

- Primary liaison between the call center operations and the project team
- Define call center operation priorities
- Manage and coordinate call center operation requirements definition
- Communicate project status to the call center operations
- Manage and coordinate all call center operation project activities
- Provide regular updates to project manager on all activities

IT Development Lead:

- Manage design, development, and testing of all internal development
- Manage and coordinate development resources
- Manage vendor development integration
- Provide regular updates to project manager on all activities

(continued)

SAMPLE Project Plan (*continued*)

IT Architecture Lead:
- Manage architecture design, development, and testing
- Manage and coordinate architecture development resources
- Manage vendor architecture development
- Provide regular updates to project manager on all activities

Vendor Project Lead:
- Insure delivery of services and products according to plan
- Manage vendor activities
- Manage vendor resources
- Escalate issues to project manager
- Provide information to other team leads
- Provide regular updates to project manager on all activities

9. Cost Management Plan

Costs will be logged in the department's project accounting system weekly, and the Project Core Team will review the reports in the Project Plan Review (PPR) meeting.

---

multiple views, each with a different purpose. For example, there are views to help you understand the relationship between tasks, scope of tasks, and status of tasks. There is also usually a resource list, which includes the cost and availability of project resources. See the following project schedule sample for more details.

⚹Requirements Definition⚹

Before you can determine which vendor best meets your requirements, you need to define your requirements. It is easier to define the requirements if you divide the task into groups of requirements and focus on each group individually. It is recommended that you focus on defining functionality, technology, strategic partnership potential, and cost requirements, each as separate groups.

Functionality Requirements

A functionality requirement is a business function or activity that the business needs to perform. The functionality requirements are a more detailed version of the business needs defined in the project charter. They too answer the question of *what* needs to happen. It is very important that you do not include the *how* it should

SAMPLE PROJECT SCHEDULE

ID	ⓘ	Task Name	Duration	Start	Finish	Pre	Owner
0		**SAMPLE PROJECT SCHEDULE**	**151 days**	**01/01/01**	**07/30/01**		
1		Project Start Date	1 day	01/01/01	01/01/01		
2		**Initiation**	**16 days**	**01/02/01**	**01/23/01**		
3		**Business Need**	**3 days**	**01/02/01**	**01/04/01**		
4		Define Business Need	2 days	01/02/01	01/03/01	1	Business Lead
5		Review Business Need	1 day	01/04/01	01/04/01	4	Business Sponsor
6		Business Need Approval	0 days	01/04/01	01/04/01	5	Business Sponsor
7		**Project Charter**	**13 days**	**01/05/01**	**01/23/01**		
8		Schedule Charter Meetings	1 day	01/05/01	01/05/01	6	Project Manager
9		Chartering Meetings	4 days	01/15/01	01/18/01	8FS+5 days	Project Manager
10		Develop Project Charter	2 days	01/19/01	01/22/01	9	Project Manager
11		Review Project Charter	1 day	01/23/01	01/23/01	10	Project Sponsor
12		Project Charter Approval	0 days	01/23/01	01/23/01	11	Project Sponsor
13		**Planning**	**15 days**	**01/24/01**	**02/13/01**		
14		**Project Plan**	**5 days**	**01/24/01**	**01/30/01**		
15		Define Project Manager	1 day	01/24/01	01/24/01	12	Project Sponsor
16		Define Project Team	1 day	01/24/01	01/24/01	12	Project Manager
17		Project Kick-off Meeting	1 day	01/25/01	01/25/01	15,16	Project Manager
18		Develop Project Plan	2 days	01/26/01	01/29/01	17	Project Manager
19		Review Project Plan	1 day	01/30/01	01/30/01	18	Project Sponsor
20		**Finalize Vendor List**	**8 days**	**01/31/01**	**02/09/01**		
21		Define Vendor List	1 day	01/31/01	01/31/01	19	Procurement Lead
22		Create RFI	1 day	02/01/01	02/01/01	21	Procurement Lead
23		Email RFI to Suppliers	1 day	02/02/01	02/02/01	22	Procurement Lead
24		Vendor RFI Response Due	0 days	02/02/01	02/02/01	23	Vendors
25		Select Vendor List	4 days	02/05/01	02/08/01	24	Project Team
26		Notify Vendors of List	1 day	02/09/01	02/09/01	25	Procurement Lead
27		**Decision Scoring Matrix**	**3 days**	**02/09/01**	**02/13/01**		
28		Establish Evaluation Criteria	1 day	02/09/01	02/09/01	25	Project Team
29		Develop Decision Scoring Matrix	1 day	02/12/01	02/12/01	28	Project Team
30		Review Decision Scoring Matrix	1 day	02/13/01	02/13/01	29	Project Sponsor
31		Decision Scoring Matrix Approval	0 days	02/13/01	02/13/01	30	Project Sponsor
32		**Research**	**24 days**	**02/14/01**	**03/19/01**		
33		**RFP Process**	**24 days**	**02/14/01**	**03/19/01**		
34		**Create RFP**	**9 days**	**02/14/01**	**02/26/01**		
35		**Create Content**	**5 days**	**02/14/01**	**02/20/01**		
36		Functional Requirements	5 days	02/14/01	02/20/01	31	Business Lead
37		Technology Requirements	5 days	02/14/01	02/20/01	31	Development Lead, Architecture Lead
38		Strategic Partnership Requirements	5 days	02/14/01	02/20/01	31	Procurement Lead
39		Cost Requirements	5 days	02/14/01	02/20/01	31	Procurement Lead
40		Appendix Info	5 days	02/14/01	02/20/01	31	Procurement Lead
41		Create Draft 1	1 day	02/21/01	02/21/01	35	Procurement Lead
42		Review Draft 1	1 day	02/22/01	02/22/01	41	Project Manager
43		Create Final Version	1 day	02/23/01	02/23/01	42	Procurement Lead
44		Review Final Version	1 day	02/26/01	02/26/01	43	Project Sponsor, Project Manager
45		RFP Approval	0 days	02/26/01	02/26/01	44	Project Sponsor
46		Send RFP to Vendors	0 days	02/26/01	02/26/01	45	Procurement Lead
47		Vendor Proposals Due	0 days	03/19/01	03/19/01	46FS+15 days	Vendors
48		**Evaluation**	**19 days**	**03/20/01**	**04/13/01**		
49		Proposal Review	3 days	03/20/01	03/22/01	47	Project Manager
50		Vendor Scoring	3 days	03/23/01	03/27/01	49	Procurement Lead
51		Team Recommendation	1 day	03/28/01	03/28/01	50	Project Manager
52		Decision Process for Short List (3 vendors)	1 day	03/29/01	03/29/01	51	Project Manager
53		Short List Evaluation	11 days	03/30/01	04/13/01		
54		Reference Calls	3 days	03/30/01	04/03/01	52	Project Manager
55		Schedule On-site Vendor Demos	1 day	03/30/01	03/30/01	52	Project Manager
56		On-site Vendor Demos	3 days	04/09/01	04/11/01	55FS+5 days	Project Manager
57		Decision Process	1 day	04/12/01	04/12/01	54,56	Project Manager
58		Communicate Decision to Vendors	1 day	04/13/01	04/13/01	57	Project Manager
59		**Negotiation**	**23 days**	**04/16/01**	**05/16/01**		
60		Negotiation Strategy	1 day	04/16/01	04/16/01	58	Procurement Lead
61		Negotiation Planning	2 days	04/17/01	04/18/01	60	Procurement Lead
62		Business Negotiations	10 days	04/19/01	05/02/01	61	Procurement Lead
63		Contract Negotiations	20 days	04/19/01	05/16/01	61	Procurement Lead
64		Contract Approval	0 days	05/16/01	05/16/01	63	Procurement Lead
65		**Implementation**	**37 days**	**05/24/01**	**07/13/01**		
66		Project Implementation Team Kick-off	1 day	05/24/01	05/24/01	64FS+5 days	Project Manager
67		Development	20 days	05/25/01	06/21/01	66	Development Lead
68		Testing	10 days	06/22/01	07/05/01	67	Development Lead
69		Training	5 days	07/06/01	07/12/01	68	Vendor, Business Lead
70		Deployment	1 day	07/13/01	07/13/01	69	Project Manager
71		**Operation**	**11 days**	**07/16/01**	**07/30/01**		
72		Transition Support to Operations	5 days	07/16/01	07/20/01	70	Project Manager
73		Project Closure	6 days	07/23/01	07/30/01		
74		Technology Acquisition Executive Summary	2 days	07/23/01	07/24/01	72	Project Manager
75		Project Team Member Reviews	3 days	07/23/01	07/25/01	72	Project Manager
76		Project Closure Form	1 day	07/23/01	07/23/01	72	Project Manager
77		Celebrate Success	1 day	07/30/01	07/30/01	70FS+10 days	Project Manager

happen at this point. You will want to leave it open for the vendor to present *how* you should accomplish each requirement.

It is important to define all the functionality requirements of the stakeholder business organizations involved. You need to know what functionality is necessary before you can evaluate which vendor is best positioned to deliver that functionality. To put this into perspective, let's look at a functionality requirement for a house as an analogy. A real estate agent should know that his buyer is disabled and has a functionality requirement for the house to have wheelchair access. If he looks for a house before knowing the buyer's functionality requirements, he risks wasting his time showing the buyer houses that do not meet the buyer's minimum requirements. Think of yourself as the real estate agent and the project team as the buyer. Make sure the project team clearly defines its functionality requirements before you start contacting vendors.

Functionality requirements are best defined in a group session with members of the stakeholder organizations. You should have someone facilitate these sessions with each stakeholder organization. The facilitator should lead the discussion by probing for more detail and questioning requirements as the stakeholders express them. The goal is to capture as much information as possible while staying on track and covering the full spectrum of requirements. The facilitator might experience some conflict between stakeholders. This is not necessarily a bad thing. Conflict can bring out the true requirements and inspire more participation. The facilitator is responsible for managing this conflict so that it continues until all sides of the argument are heard while ensuring that the conflict stays professional.

Functionality requirements can be captured in many different formats. Some prefer a format such as the following bulleted list.

Tender transaction:

- Accept Visa, MasterCard, American Express, and Discover

- Accept debit cards

- Accept cash

- Accept checks

- Accept multiple payment methods

Another way to present the functionality requirements is in a table format as in Table 2-1. The table approach is recommended, as it is easier to add the requirements to a Request for Proposal (RFP). See Chapter 3 for more information.

Table 2-1: Categorized Table of Requirements

#	Category	Requirement
1	Tender Transaction	Accept Visa, MasterCard, American Express, and Discover
2	Tender Transaction	Accept debit transactions
3	Tender Transaction	Accept cash
4	Tender Transaction	Accept checks
5	Tender Transaction	Accept multiple payment methods
6	Tender Transaction	Void transactions

The level of detail required in defining functionality requirements should be as specific as possible. Remember, the more explicit you are in defining your requirements for the vendor, the better chance the vendor will have in proposing an appropriate solution. To get an idea of the level of detail necessary, see the sample RFP in Chapter 3.

Once you have defined all the functionality requirements for the proposed solution, you need to present them for approval. Typically, you need approval from the stakeholder business organizations, the project manager, and the project sponsor (usually in that order). Be sure to have everyone sign off on this document to ensure that all stakeholders agree on the functionality requirements.

Technology Requirements

The technology requirements are different than the functionality requirements in that there are usually fewer options for a vendor's response. These requirements are more black and white. The vendor's technology either meets the requirement or it doesn't. For example, a technology requirement might be compatibility with a specific network operating system. The vendor's product is either compatible with the network operating system or it isn't. Because the technology requirements are as such, it is easier to compare vendors and their abilities to meet these types of requirements.

It is very important to define your organization's technology requirements. Failure to do so can result in the purchase of technology that will not work in your computing environment. A product with a poor technology base can also limit its ability to adapt to your ever-changing business.

Defining technology requirements is a lot easier than defining functionality requirements. In fact, most IT organizations will already have their technology requirements defined. A full set of technology requirements can be applied to multiple technology development and acquisition projects. Have the technology analysts on your team do a little checking around. They will probably find a set of technology requirements that were used on a different project that would also be sufficient for your project. If not, have your technology analysts work with each organization's IT department to gather technology requirements. The format for documenting technology requirements should be the same as the format used in documenting the functionality requirements.

Once you have a full set of technology requirements, you need to obtain approval from the IT management. Make sure that management signs the requirements document so that you have covered all the bases and have included the right people in the process. See the sample RFP in Chapter 3 for an example of a set of technology requirements.

Strategic Partnership Requirements

Conducting a technology acquisition project every year would be very costly. Therefore, you should do your best to select a vendor and a technology that can grow with your business for the next 2–3 years. Before you begin a business relationship with a vendor, make sure that the vendor meets your requirements as a business partner.

Determine what your expectations of a technology vendor are before you begin researching and evaluating vendors. Decide what type of company will work well with your company. Figure out if you are looking for a technology driven organization or a market driven organization. A technology driven organization is focused on having the latest and greatest technology, but may not want to change its technology for each customer. Providing the best technology is its focus and what it does best. A market driven company, on the other hand, puts the customer before the technology. Its primary focus is to meet each of its customer's requirements, even at the expense of providing leading-edge technology. Some companies work better with one type of vendor than another. Determine which type will be best for your company in the long term. Also, be sure to ask the vendor how much its base solution can be customized to meet your needs without limiting your ability to take advantage of future upgrades.

The strategic partnership requirements should be defined by a subset of the project team. If you plan to travel to vendor locations or the vendor's customer locations, you will need all of these people to attend each visit. For this reason, you will want to minimize the number of project team members while ensuring all areas are represented. In past projects that I have managed, all project team members were included because each member represented an important stakeholder organization. The extra costs were worth it because we planned to partner with the selected vendor for the next 2 to 3 years. Regardless of the number of people involved in the strategic partnership requirement development, it is recommended that you include all of them in every research method that is associated with these requirements. This allows them to evaluate each vendor fairly during the Evaluation phase.

The format for documenting strategic partnership requirements can be as simple as a list of questions for the vendor to answer.

When you are defining your strategic partnership requirements, it is recommended that you cover the following areas by asking these questions:

- *Vendor profile:* What type of company do you want to do business with? This can apply to the company's size (revenue, market share, employees, and products), priorities, partnerships, certifications, or any other characteristic that you feel is important.

- *Training:* What are your training requirements for the vendor? Do you need the vendor to train your trainers or conduct the training for you? Is it important that your vendor have significant training capabilities? What are your expectations for the vendor's training capability?

- *Support:* What are your support requirements? Will you need the vendor to support the end users of the product or your internal support personnel? What are your Service Level Agreement (SLA) requirements? Do you have any preferences in the method of training used (training session, training manual, or computer-based training)?

- *Experience:* Is it important that the vendor be well established in its market, or is it OK if the vendor is a newcomer? Some organizations will not deal with vendors who are not well established within their market. How leading edge does the technology need to be? You will have more vendors to chose from if a mature technology is sufficient in addressing the business need.

- *Thought leadership:* Do you want a vendor to take the lead in telling you what you should be doing or will you be telling the vendor what you want it to do? If you already know specifically what you want, you might not require a vendor with significant creative design consulting capabilities.

- *Customer references:* How important are customer references? Is it important that the vendor have experience with implementations in similar businesses?

Once you have a full set of strategic partner requirements, you need to obtain approval from the stakeholder organizations, project manager, and project sponsor. Make sure they sign the requirements document so that you have covered all the bases and have included the right people in the process. See the sample RFP in Chapter 3 for a list of strategic partnership requirements.

Cost Requirements

Determine your cost requirements for the technology acquisition and decide whether the cost is a high priority in the decision to choose a vendor. It is important to define your cost requirements prior to seeing a vendor's price quote. This is similar to determining how much you plan to spend prior to going shopping. Predetermining cost requirements will make it easier to focus on the costs that were used in the business case, a document used to determine the financial costs, benefits, and return on investment for the project.

It is helpful to create a spreadsheet with the cost model so that vendors can fill in their numbers using the same format. This allows for easier comparison.

Cost requirements should be defined by the project manager and be reviewed for approval by the project sponsor. In some cases, you may also need to include a representative from a stakeholder organization that is supplying the majority of the budget for the acquisition. The general rule is to stick with the costs outlined in the business case for the solution.

Once you have defined the cost requirements, you need to obtain approval from the stakeholder organizations, project manager, and project sponsor. Make sure they sign the requirements document so that you have covered all the bases and have included the right people in the process. See the sample RFP in Chapter 3 for an example of cost requirements.

Prioritization

It is common to find that each vendor has strong points and weak points. Where one vendor is exceptional, another might be lacking. For example, one vendor may have a better architecture but is a small and unstable company financially. Another vendor may have a weak architecture but a strong and stable company financially. Which do you choose? Either way, you are at risk. This type of situation reinforces the need to prioritize your requirements prior to researching and evaluating vendors. By understanding what is important to your organization before looking at vendors, you can be objective about what is important. On the other hand, if you don't have a good understanding of your organization's priorities, you may end up selecting the wrong vendor.

Defining the Priorities

The members of the project team should define the priorities for their area of expertise. In other words, the business subject matter experts (SMEs) should prioritize the functionality requirements, technology analysts should prioritize the technology requirements, team members involved in evaluating strategic partnership potential should prioritize the strategic partnership requirements, and the project manager and project sponsor should prioritize cost requirements. Each of these team members should prioritize their requirements in order of importance. Once this is complete, you should meet with your project sponsor and managers from the project stakeholder organizations to have them prioritize at a higher level (see the following decision scoring matrix template). After accomplishing these two prioritization tasks, work to combine them to understand how the high-level priorities integrate with the detailed level priorities. The decision scoring matrix is a tool I highly recommend that you use to prioritize your requirements.

Start by listing the requirement categories (functionality, technology, strategic partnership, and cost) and dividing 100 points among them. One hundred points works well because it represents 100 percent of the decision. This makes it easier to conceptualize the percentage of the decision that will be allocated to each category. As you assign points to a requirement category, those points become the percentage of the decision that will be decided by how the vendors rate in that category. For example, if cost is not the primary concern, you might assign 10 points to this category. This would mean that the cost of each vendor's solution represents 10 percent of the decision (see the following decision scoring matrix template and sample).

Once you have divided the 100 points into the four categories, you can then proceed to divide the points in each category to the subgroups of requirements. Using the preceding cost category example, you might have two subgroups under cost requirements called initial costs and annual support costs. If your stakeholders and project sponsors stress minimizing the company's ongoing expenses, you might assign 7 of the 10 points to annual support costs, which are expense costs, and 3 of the 10 points to the initial cost, which is usually a capital cost. In this scenario, the ongoing cost represents 7 percent of the final decision of which vendor best meets your requirements. Continue assigning points from each category to the subgroups within that category until all points are assigned to a subgroup. This information should be documented in a format similar to the decision scoring matrix.

Template

TEMPLATE: DECISION SCORING MATRIX

The decision scoring matrix is a table that helps to objectify the decision-making process by breaking the overall decision into many small decisions. Although this may not always produce the final decision, it will definitely tell you a lot about how the vendors compare so that you can make an educated decision. The following table can be used as a template for the decision scoring matrix.

	Category Points	Group Points	Vendor A	Vendor B	Vendor C
Functionality	30				
<Requirement group>		10	8	4	9
<Requirement group>		15	10	11	10
<Requirement group>		5	5	5	5
Technology	40				
<Requirement group>		15	10	1	5
<Requirement group>		10	10	5	10
<Requirement group>		15	12	7	10
Strategic Partnership Potential	20				
<Requirement group>		10	8	10	8
<Requirement group>		10	5	10	8
Costs	10				
<Requirement group>		4	2	4	2
<Requirement group>		6	3	6	2
Totals	100	100	73	63	69

As you can see from the totals, Vendor A would represent the vendor who is more closely aligned with your company's requirements.

The following sample decision scoring matrix was used in a real technology acquisition. The sample was modified to protect the confidentiality of the vendors, but you can see the amount of detail that this tool can provide to the decision makers. In this

SAMPLE DECISION SCORING MATRIX

EXAMPLE SCORING MATRIX Key: 0-Doesn't Meet, 1-Weak Meets, 2-Meets, 3-Strong Meets, 4-Exceeds

VERSION 4.0 - DATED 11/13/2000 1PM

Description	Points	% of Points	Vendor A Score	Vendor A Points	Vendor B Score	Vendor B Points	Vendor C Score	Vendor C Points	Vendor D Score	Vendor D Points
Functionality	10									
1 Functionality Group 1		5.0%	3	0.4	4	0.5	1.5	0.2	3	0.4
2 Functionality Group 2		5.0%	2	0.3	4	0.5	3	0.4	1	0.1
3 Functionality Group 3		2.0%	3.5	0.2	2	0.1	0	0.0	0	0.0
4 Functionality Group 4		15.0%	1	0.4	3	1.1	2	0.8	2	0.8
5 Functionality Group 5		15.0%	3	1.1	4	1.5	2	0.8	2	0.8
6 Functionality Group 6		15.0%	2	0.8	2	0.8	2	0.8	0	0.0
7 Functionality Group 7		15.0%	3	1.1	4	1.5	3	1.1	2	0.8
8 Functionality Group 8		8.0%	1	0.2	4	0.8	2.5	0.5	1	0.2
9 Functionality Group 9		7.0%	2	0.4	3	0.5	0.5	0.1	0	0.0
10 Functionality Group 10		5.0%	1	0.1	4	0.5	2	0.3	2	0.3
11 Functionality Group 11		5.0%	1	0.1	2	0.3	3	0.4	2	0.3
12 Functionality Group 12		3.0%	1	0.1	4	0.3	1	0.1	1	0.1
				5.1		**8.4**		**5.2**		**3.5**
Technology	30									
1 Technology Requirements Group 1		12.0%	4	3.6	2	1.8	3	2.7	2	1.8
2 Technology Requirements Group 2		7.5%	3	1.7	3	1.7	2	1.1	0	0.0
3 Technology Requirements Group 3		5.0%	4	1.5	2	0.8	2	0.8	2	0.8
4 Technology Requirements Group 4		5.0%	3	1.1	0	0.0	2	0.8	1	0.4
5 Technology Requirements Group 5		7.5%	3	1.7	1	0.6	1	0.6	1	0.6
6 Technology Requirements Group 6		7.5%	2	1.1	3	1.7	2	1.1	0	0.0
7 Technology Requirements Group 7		17.0%	4	5.1	4	5.1	2	2.6	1	1.3
8 Technology Requirements Group 8		17.0%	3	3.8	1	1.3	0	0.0	1	1.3
9 Technology Requirements Group 9		12.0%	4	3.6	3	2.7	2	1.8	2	1.8
10 Technology Requirements Group 10		12.0%	3	2.7	4	3.6	2	1.8	1	0.9
11 Technology Requirements Group 11		5.0%	4	1.5	2	0.8	1	0.4	2	0.8
12 Technology Requirements Group 12		0.0%	3	0.0	3	0.0	1	0.0	1	0.0
13 Technology Requirements Group 13		0.0%	3	0.0	2	0.0	1	0.0	1	0.0
				27.5		**19.9**		**13.5**		**9.5**
Strategic Partnership Potential	20									
1 Supplier Profile		10.0%	3	1.5	4	2.0	2	1.0	1	0.5
2 Training		20.0%	3	3.0	2.5	2.5	2	2.0	1	1.0
3 Support		20.0%	3	3.0	4	4.0	1	1.0	2	2.0
4 Experience		20.0%	3	3.0	3	3.0	2	2.0	1	1.0
5 Implementation Plan		10.0%	2	1.0	4	2.0	2	1.0	0	0.0
6 Customer Reference Calls		20.0%	2	2.0	4	4.0	0	0.0	0	0.0
				13.5		**17.5**		**7.0**		**4.5**
Costs	40									
1 Initial Costs - Area 1		57.0%	4	22.8	3	17.1		0.0		0.0
2 Initial Costs - Area 2		10.0%	3	3.0	1	1.0				
3 Initial Costs - Area 3		15.0%	4	6.0	2	3.0				
4 Initial Costs - Area 4		11.0%	1.5	1.7	2	2.2				
5 Ongoing Costs - Area 1		3.0%	4	1.2	3	0.9				
6 Ongoing Costs - Area 2		3.0%	2	0.6	1	0.3				
7 Ongoing Costs - Area 3		1.0%	1.5	0.2	2.5	0.3		0.0		0.0
				35.4		**24.8**		**0.0**		**0.0**
Total Score	100			**81.4**		**70.5**		**25.8**		**17.5**

39

sample, you can see that Vendor A is clearly the leader in technology and cost, whereas Vendor B is the leader in functionality and strategic partnership potential. Because technology and cost were given more weight in the scoring, Vendor A became the vendor of choice. Using this tool, you can see how it can help you break down a substantial decision into several small decisions.

Approval and Consensus of the Priorities

Once you have reviewed the final list of priorities and have defined a decision scoring matrix, you need to obtain approval from the project sponsor and project stakeholder organizations. It is usually surprising to find out that priorities are different than initially communicated when it comes down to objectively defining and documenting these priorities. For example, you may hear at the outset of the project planning that cost is critical in selecting a new system. However, when you ask project stakeholders to suggest a trade-off in functionality for cost in the decision scoring matrix, they tend to change their minds and usually allocate a higher percentage to functionality than cost—hence the value of the decision scoring matrix. It forces the decision makers to quantitatively prioritize what is important in the decision to choose a vendor. Take the time to do a quality job defining the priorities and gaining a consensus, and you will greatly improve your project's probability of success in selecting the right vendor and technology for your business needs.

You should also consider the impact that hidden agendas can have on the decision-making priorities. Try to get a good understanding of the reasons behind the priorities. If you sense that priorities don't agree with the business need and business case that justified the project to begin with, it is important to pursue your hunch and gain an understanding of why the priorities have changed. There are cases where managers undertake practices often referred to as "empire building" at the expense of what is right for the company. Although you might not always be able to stop these hidden agendas, it is important that the project manager and project sponsor both be aware of the influence these agendas will have on the success of the project.

It is highly recommended that you obtain a signature from all stakeholders approving the priorities stated in the decision scoring matrix. Although this can seem a little excessive, it is important because it causes the decision makers to perform due diligence in making sure they have correctly defined their priorities.

Defining the Solution

Once the business need has been analyzed and approved, it is then time to begin defining a solution. Before proceeding, make sure you understand all of the business drivers behind the need. Additionally, make sure you have a good understanding of all the facts and assumptions surrounding the business need. Once you are confident that you have a good understanding of the business need, you can define potential solutions. There are several ways to define potential solutions including defining them internally, leveraging internal best practices, evaluating industry best practices, or hiring an outside expert to define potential solutions (Figure 2-2).

- *Defining solutions internally:* The most common approach to defining potential solutions is to do it internally. Most companies have business analysts and technical analysts who have an extensive understanding of the business and current technology. Bringing these two groups together can often produce the best solutions to address the business need. If you pursue this approach, have an objective person facilitate the discussion. A good facilitator will keep the discussion on track while drawing out all of the possible solutions. It is important for the facilitator to understand how to manage conflict to engage the group while respecting all attendees as equals. It is sometimes helpful to conduct these sessions off-site to keep everyone focused on the task and eliminate distractions.

- *Evaluating internal best practices:* Find out if your organization captures best practices. If your business is a subsidiary of a parent company, you may find that another subsidiary of the parent company has already captured a best practice for addressing the business need. This can be one of the most efficient methods for defining a solution to address the business need.

- *Evaluating industry best practices:* Another approach to defining potential solutions is to evaluate industry best practices. This is typically done with the help of a third-party research firm. You can also leverage your staff's contacts at other companies to research industry best practices. You will find that most companies that are not in competition with your company will be happy to share best and worst practices with you if you do the same. You might also be able to acquire industry best practices from a consulting firm that specializes in your business. Evaluating industry best practices allows you to leverage time and money spent as well as the lessons learned by other companies to help you define the potential solutions for your business need. You will also have a better understanding of which vendors are experienced in providing solutions for your business need.

• *Hiring an external expert to define solutions:* In the previous approach, you acquire a set of industry best practices that have already been developed. In this approach, you hire an expert to define solutions that have not yet been developed. Although this approach can be very expensive, hiring an expert can also provide an objective list of potential solutions that you may not have been able to define internally. The key is to hire the right expert. An expert must have extensive experience in your industry and have a history of successes in addressing real business needs for similar companies.

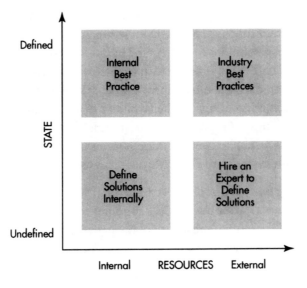

Figure 2-2: Four methods for identifying potential solutions

Upon completing your list of potential solutions to address the business need, you need to begin the process of selecting a solution. At this point in the process, the key is not to make the final decision. Instead, you should decide on which solution to spend the additional time and resources that are required to develop a detailed business case.

One of the major assumptions of this book is that you have identified technology as the solution to address your business need. If technology is the solution, the next step is to determine where the technology will come from. There has been much debate on the question of when to buy and when to build technology. What is the correct answer? There is no universally correct answer to this question. However, answering the following 10 questions will help you determine the correct solution for your current situation:

1. *Will the technology provide a competitive advantage?* Building technology requires your company's time and resources to manage, build, implement, and support that technology. Are you willing to commit your staff to this effort or is there a better use of their time? You are better off dedicating your limited staff to building technology that will give you an advantage over your competitors and buying technology that won't.

   Developing an accounting system is an example of a technology that will not give most businesses a competitive advantage. There are literally hundreds of accounting system vendors in the marketplace that have dedicated huge research and development (R&D) budgets to fine-tuning these systems to support any type of enterprise. Don't focus your time and energies on reinventing the wheel when it will not put you in any better position than if you had purchased the system.

   An example of a system that will give most businesses a competitive advantage if developed internally is a call-tracking system. Most businesses can provide unique support options to their customers by building a custom call-tracking system. Although there are generic call-tracking systems on the market, you know your customers best and would probably be able to create a customized system that would provide better support than your competitors.

2. *Can you build it?* The demand for quality technology professionals is rapidly increasing. This demand is making it more difficult to retain quality personnel who can build the technology you need efficiently and effectively. Technology vendors are dedicated to hiring and retaining the most talented technology professionals. The quality of their technology resources might enable them to build a better product in less time and at a lower cost. Look at the quality of the work that your internal IT professionals are producing. Are projects delivered on time, within budget, and with the desired functionality and level of quality?

3. *Can you build it for less money?* Determine how mature the market is for this technology. If there are only a few vendors in the market, they might be able to charge excessive prices and get away with it due to lack of alternatives for the customer. In this case, you might be able to save a significant amount of money by building the technology yourself.

   On the other hand, if there is significant competition among vendors in this market, you might be able to buy a technology at a much lower price than you could build it for yourself. This is generally because vendors are spreading the cost of R&D over all their customers, whereas you would only be able to absorb this cost within your own business.

4. *Can you build it fast enough?* Determine how critical this technology is to your business, what the Return on Investment (ROI) is, and how much it is costing you not to have this technology. You might find that it is more beneficial to have the technology sooner than later, even if it costs more. In this case, you can implement an existing vendor system faster than you can design, build, test, and implement one yourself.

5. *Is this the best use for your internal technology resources?* Determine what skill sets your technology professionals have. If your technology resources are experienced in building mainframe systems and the situation calls for a client/server system, you will save in training time and cost as well as avoid mistakes of inexperience if you buy the technology.

6. *Are you willing to take on the risk of building it yourself?* Vendors are committed to delivering a solution as agreed to in a legally binding contract. If they can't deliver, they take the hit on the development costs. They assume all the risks in this situation. When you build a system yourself, you assume the risk of losing time and resources if the solution cannot be implemented successfully.

7. *Can you provide adequate support and upgrades after implementation?* Determine how effective and responsive your support department is. Decide whether it can provide the same or better support than a vendor or if it can provide support for less money. Some organizations are so overextended that they cannot assume support of an additional system and provide the same quality of support as a vendor.

    Establish whether you can provide upgrades and enhancements to the system quarterly or twice a year. It is inevitable that users of the system will have additional requirements that they couldn't have defined prior to using the system. Determine if your organization can continually provide improvements at the same rate as a vendor whose bottom line is directly tied to its ability to improve the product.

8. *Is building technology part of your core competency?* Many businesses are achieving positive results by focusing on their core competency and

outsourcing development and management of anything that is not tied directly to it. Establish your company's stance on buying or building technology. Figure out if your company is trying to do too many things at one time.

9. *Where is the technology headed in the future?* You might be able to build technology that is equivalent to what is available on the market today, but do you know what products are just about to hit the market? Vendors may have been working on new versions of their products that are far superior to what is currently on the market. If you build it yourself, you may find out about a new product after you have invested a great deal in building your own solution.

   You may also find that vendors are heading in the wrong direction with the technology and feel confident that your organization can build a superior system.

10. *What are your competitors doing?* Determine if your competitors are buying or building this technology. If they are buying it, find out who they are buying it from. If they aren't focusing significant capital in this technology, you can either do the same or try to implement technology that can differentiate you from them. If your competitors bought their technology, you may learn a lot about their technology during the Research phase of a technology acquisition process just by evaluating their vendor's product.

    It is not always an easy task find out which vendor's technology your competitors are using. One way that has been effective for me in the past is to look at their job postings to see what technology they are hiring developers for. You can also check their press releases and the vendors' press releases to see if there were any announcements regarding their selection of a vendor for a given technology. If all else fails, ask the vendors or industry consultants. If they are not tied to any confidentiality agreements with your competitors, they will usually share this information.

    Table 2.2 summarizes the preceding 10 questions and is provided as a quick reference.

Table 2-2: Ten Questions for the Buy versus Build Decision

Question	Description
Will the technology provide a competitive advantage?	Are you willing to commit your resources to this effort or is there a better use of their time?
Can you build it?	Do your resources have the capability and successful track record for this type of development project?
Can you build it for less money?	Can you build it for less money than the vendors are currently charging?
Can you build it fast enough?	Can you build it fast enough to meet the business need? The ROI for the solution may be great enough to justify buying instead of building.
Is this the best use for your internal technology resources?	Is there another initiative that would be a better use of your internal resources?
Are you willing to take on the risk of building it yourself?	Can you afford to take the risk of project delays and cost overruns?
Can you provide adequate support and upgrades after implementation?	Can you adequately support the solution? Additionally, can you commit to providing regular updates after the initial implementation?
Is building technology part of your core competency?	Do you want to be in the business of building technology? What is the core competency of the company?
Where is the technology headed in the future?	Are you sure that the vendors are not working on new technologies that you could not possibly build yourself?
What are your competitors doing?	Are your competitors buying or building this technology? Is there a competitive advantage in taking a different approach?

Answering the preceding 10 questions will help you decide whether to buy or build the solution to address your business need. This will not be an easy decision, but it is critical that you make a wise decision. I have been involved in projects where the decision to build proved to be the wrong one, which cost the company tens of millions of dollars and years in wasted effort. On the other hand, I have also seen a company's decision to buy technology prove more costly than it would have been to build it themselves.

It is also very common for a project to consist of a combination of buying and building a technology. For example, you may buy architecture components, such as databases, network operating systems, and hardware, and then build the applications that use these architecture components. Remember to answer the previous 10 questions for each purchase to ensure that you are buying or building for the right reasons.

The decision to buy or build is usually made by the project sponsor. Regardless of who makes the decision, the decision maker will usually make a preliminary decision and then require that a business case be developed before making the final decision. The business case will provide the detailed analysis to ensure that the solution is justified. Many assumptions will need to be made, such as the cost of buying the solution. It is very important to document all of the assumptions that are made in developing a business case for a given solution. This will help the decision maker understand the risks that are involved in pursuing the solution.

Once the project sponsor is satisfied with the contents of the business case, he will usually take it to the executive sponsors for final approval. In some organizations, the executive sponsors make the final decision to proceed with a solution. In others, this decision is delegated to the project sponsor.

For the purposes of this book, let's assume that you will be buying a solution. The remainder of the book will provide a framework for managing a technology acquisition project.

Identifying and Contacting Vendors

Another key activity in the Planning phase is to identify which vendors you will include in the technology acquisition. Although this sounds pretty easy, it's not always as easy as you might imagine. Some technologies have hundreds of vendors; others only have a few.

There are many ways to identify prospective vendors. The following list contains some of the common ways to identify possible vendors:

- *Industry experts:* There may be consulting firms that specialize in the industry. Hiring a consultant to provide expertise during the acquisition process can save you time by letting you know which vendors definitely cannot meet your requirements and which ones can.

- *Research firms:* There are many firms that specialize in researching industries, markets, companies, and technologies. They sell this research to other companies. Although this information can be expensive initially, it can save you money in the long run if it saves you the time and money associated with evaluating a vendor that doesn't even come close to meeting your requirements.

- *Word of mouth:* You can find out who the players are in the industry by calling your network of contacts and asking them to recommend vendors that you should include in your research. Although this information is usually very subjective, it can be helpful in identifying prospective vendors.

- *Past experience:* Have you or any other members of your company worked with this technology in the past? Try to find others in your company who have been through a technology acquisition for this particular technology at a previous company. They will be able to provide you with some valuable insight in identifying prospective vendors.

- *Magazine articles:* Industry trade magazines often evaluate specific technologies. Although you shouldn't assume that these articles are objective and fair, they can help you identify the players that should be considered in your technology acquisition project.

- *Internet:* The Internet can also be a valuable tool for identifying prospective vendors. Companies that have a viable, appropriate technology will have a Web site with information about their company, products, services, and customers. You can also find online industry magazines and research firms that have a significant amount of free information available.

- *Other Companies:* If you have contacts from other companies that have recently been through the process of acquiring the same technology, you might ask them which vendors they included in their acquisition process.

Use as many avenues as you reasonably can in a short period of time to identify the list of vendors that should be included in your technology acquisition process. The key is to identify all vendors that can meet your requirements while keeping the list down to a manageable number.

TIPS: NUMBER OF VENDORS

✔ You should identify a manageable list of prospective vendors without limiting yourself or omitting a vendor that might be the best vendor for your requirements. In my experience, more than 10 is too many, and less than three is too few. My preference is to start with six and after proposals are returned, narrow the list to three.

✔ Three is the minimum number of vendors that you should enter into the Evaluation and Negotiation phases. If you end up eliminating a vendor from the final three, you never want to put yourself in a situation where there is only one vendor remaining. This will eliminate your leverage if the remaining vendor finds out it is the only choice you have.

There are times when it will be impossible to find a vendor with technology that can meet all of your requirements. In this case, you might need to look at multiple vendors working in partnerships. For example, you might find that there are vendors that can develop the technology but are too small to implement the solution. In this situation, you may decide to approach some of the larger, more capable consulting firms to take the lead and present a total solution including one or more of their partner companies. The important thing when taking this approach is to make it clear who is in the lead role and not let the partner companies bypass the lead consulting firm to deal with you directly.

As soon as you have a list of prospective vendors that will be included in the process, you need to start contacting them to find out if they are interested in participating in the process. The initial contact is typically made with a phone call or letter expressing an interest to involve them in a technology acquisition process. I prefer sending a letter addressed to the head of the sales organization. This allows the vendor to either decline quickly or assign the sales effort to the proper account manager. The initial letter is called an LOI.

You may also decide to send what is called a Request for Information (RFI) along with the LOI. The RFI is a formal request similar to an RFP, but with less obligation to buy. This document can be a list of knock-out criteria that will help eliminate vendors that do not meet your most critical requirements. The RFI is a good tool to use when you have a large number of prospective vendors. It allows you to trim down the list while providing a fair chance for all vendors to participate. The RFI can also be used solely to gather information.

The purpose of the LOI is to state your intent to purchase the technology from the vendor. You should also request an LOI from the vendor stating its intent to participate in the acquisition process. The LOI usually includes the following information:

- A brief introduction of who you are and the purpose of the letter

- A statement that you are beginning a technology acquisition process and are inquiring to see if the vendor is interested in competing for your business

- A high-level outline of the business need and desired solution

You should consider sending a Non-Disclosure Agreement (NDA) to each vendor. The NDA is also commonly referred to as a confidentiality agreement. The purpose of an NDA is to protect both companies from disclosing confidential information. Be sure to send an NDA to all vendors before providing them with any confidential information about your company. If they are unwilling to sign an NDA, you need to work with the executive management and legal staff to determine whether to assume the risks associated with sharing confidential information without legal protection.

An NDA is a legal document, so you should have your company's legal representative develop and approve it. An NDA includes legal terminology that, in effect, states that the vendor cannot share information about your company to other companies without your written permission. It may also be written as a two-way NDA, meaning that you cannot share information about the vendor to other companies either. Regardless of which type of NDA your legal staff chooses, it's a good idea to have a valid NDA to protect your company from confidentiality issues.

The following checklist is provided as an aid to help you complete the tasks necessary for the Planning process.

PLANNING PROCESS CHECKLIST

❑ *Requirements have been clearly defined and documented by the project team.*

❑ *Requirements have been prioritized and documented.*

❑ *A project plan has been developed.*

❑ *All potential solutions have been identified and evaluated.*

❑ *A solution has been selected.*

❑ *The buy versus build decision has been made.*

❑ *The initial list of vendors is defined.*

❑ *Vendors have been contacted and have signed Non-Disclosure Agreements.*

THE PROJECT TEAM

What is the ideal number of resources for a technology acquisition project team? This all depends on the size and scope of your organization and the technology being acquired. For example, acquiring an accounting system for a multibillion dollar company would require more resources than acquiring an accounting system for a small law firm with 30 employees.

Although the number of resources required varies, usually the ideal team consists of six to eight people. This is a manageable number of resources and enough to provide adequate representation. If you have more than eight people on a team, it can be difficult to manage interactions with the vendors, and it can be even more difficult to reach a decision. Although I recommend no more than eight, you should have enough people to adequately represent each stakeholder business organization. You will also need to account for any third-party resources, such as consultants, contractors, or external research organizations.

Be sure to include planning for the physical resource requirements of your project. For example, will you need to reserve any off-site locations for meetings? Will you be traveling to visit vendors or their customers? Take the time to plan ahead for all resources and costs involved in the technology acquisition. This is an important part of project management and should be included in resource planning.

Project Team Roles

Decide on who you should include on your project team. The members you choose depends on many variables (for example, size of project, number of stakeholders, type of technology, and so on). The following list contains some of the key roles that must be represented:

- *Project manager:* Project managers come from many different backgrounds. It's pretty safe to say that most people have managed some kind of project at some time in their professional lives. Although managing a project does not require any specific skill set, an understanding of project management fundamentals will significantly improve the probability of success. Along with an understanding of the fundamentals, experience managing similar projects is a big plus. For those serious about project management as a profession, the fundamentals and experience of applying those fundamentals are essential. In general, some of the important qualities desired in a project manager are leadership, organization, motivation, negotiation, and communication skills.

The role of the project manager is to lead and manage a team of resources in an effort to accomplish the objectives of the project. Project managers are primarily focused on planning, executing, and controlling the activities required to accomplish the project objectives. Managing a technology acquisition will take the majority of a project manager's time.

- *Business subject matter expert (SME):* A business SME is someone selected by a stakeholder business organization to represent its requirements on the project team. This is usually a person who has been in the business unit for an extended period of time and is considered very knowledgeable about all aspects of the work that is performed in the business unit.

  The role of the business SME is to represent his or her business organization's requirements on the project team. A technology acquisition will most likely require about 25 to 50 percent of the business SME's time throughout the Research and Evaluation phases.

- *Technology analyst:* Technology analysts consist of technical experts from many different areas within an IT organization. They can be systems analysts, programmer analysts, data analysts, application architects, data architects, network communication architects, or can hold many of the other titles within an IT organization.

  The role of the technology analyst is to define technology requirements and evaluate each vendor's ability to meet those requirements. A technology acquisition will most likely require about 25 to 50 percent of the technology analyst's time throughout the Research and Evaluation phases.

  Be sure to have representation of each area within your IT organization. One person may represent more than one area, but it is essential that all areas be covered. At a minimum, I recommend you have expertise in application development, database, network, and telecommunication technologies. If you have to choose one, select a technology architecture analyst who can ensure that the vendor's technology has a solid architecture to build upon.

- *Contract administrator:* The contract administrator specializes in working with vendors and the company's legal department to create and maintain contract documentation. This position can reside within a single centralized organization or be spread out within each organization.

  The role of the contract administrator is to ensure that all contracts meet quality standards, track contract additions and changes, and facilitate contract negotiations to ensure that the contracts represent the best interests of the organization. The Negotiation phase only requires about 25 percent of the contract administrator's time.

Make sure you have your contract administrator assigned as early as possible. In addition, ensure that he has reserved adequate time on his schedule to participate in the Negotiation phase. I have had contract administrators hold up negotiations for weeks because they were involved in too many contract negotiations at one time. Take the time early on to secure his time and keep this from happening in your negotiation.

- *Legal representative:* Legal representation consists of lawyers who represent your company in legal matters. They can be internal lawyers or contracted external lawyers.

    The role of the legal representative is to ensure that the contracts are sufficient to establish the terms of the deal and minimize the risk to the organization. Because legal advice is expensive, you will want to minimize the use of these resources.

    Make sure you reserve the legal representative's time as early as possible and plan the legal contract reviews well in advance. This will allow the representative to adjust his schedule and reduce the chance of delays.

On some projects, you will find a large project team with several people playing each of the roles previously listed. In other projects, resource limitations will require people to play multiple roles. Table 2-3 illustrates some of the roles that can be combined and when it is appropriate to combine these roles.

Identifying Good Resources

The best project team member for a technology acquisition is one who is open-minded, objective, respected by his peers, professional, knowledgeable, and easy to get along with. An explanation of why each of these traits is important follows.

It is very likely that the business SMEs will have used one of the technologies being evaluated in your acquisition process. Find out how they feel about this technology and vendor. If they have a strong opinion either way, they might not be able to keep an open mind when evaluating other vendors. I once had a business SME on one of my technology acquisitions who had a strong relationship with the vendor that we had been using for the previous three years. He was very adamant that we were wasting our time and that the current vendor was the best in the market.

Table 2-3: Combining Project Team Roles

Roles Combined	When Appropriate
All roles combined	Small company atmosphere Short timeframe Extremely limited resources Application with little impact to company's success
Project Manager and Business SME	Single stakeholder organization will use technology
Project Manager and Technology Analyst	Primarily technology architecture project Multiple-stakeholder organizations will use technology
Contract Administrator and any other role	When resources are limited Contract Administrator role doesn't exist within company

I asked him if he could give the other vendors a fair chance. He said he would, but was sure that he was right. By the end of the Evaluation phase, he had come full circle and was emphasizing the downsides of the current vendor and promoting going with another vendor. Fortunately, he didn't let his ego get in the way of doing what was right for the company. Although I was lucky, you would be wise to proceed with caution when faced with a business SME that is not very open-minded.

Can the team members be objective? Remember that one of the primary reasons that you are conducting a thorough technology acquisition process is to objectify a subjective decision as much as possible. Ask questions to find out if your team members make decisions objectively or subjectively. A good example of the type of question to ask is what kind of car they last purchased and why they chose that car over other cars. If they based their decision on the feeling it gave them or what other people have told them, beware. They will probably base their decisions on the same criteria in a technology acquisition. On the other hand, if they start rattling off miles per gallon, safety ratings, horsepower, or other figures that played in their decision, you have some winners. Make sure you keep them on your project team.

Do their peers respect them? Because they will be representing their departments in the decision-making process, be sure that their departments will respect their decisions. Having respected team members support a decision will help others support the decision as well. They are the ones who will have to go back to their business organizations after the technology is selected and help sell the decision to the staff. If you select someone who is not respected by his or her peers, you might run into a lot of resistance to the final decision.

During the technology acquisition process, the project team will be representing your company with many vendors and their customers. The last thing you want to do is embarrass your company with an obnoxious or unprofessional team member (see the following case study for an example). It is not uncommon for a vendor to host your project team for lunch or dinner at some time during the acquisition process. I recommend declining these social meetings until after a vendor is selected and contracts are signed. The exception is when you are traveling with the vendor to a customer site or visiting the vendor's headquarters. In this case, it is appropriate for the vendor to take the project team out on a social function. The following case study illustrates the impact that an unprofessional project team member can have on the relationship with the vendors.

Case Study
UNPROFESSIONAL TEAM MEMBERS

On one of Jack's previous acquisition projects, a vendor had taken a few members of the project team out to dinner. After a few drinks, a couple of his team members started bashing XYZ Corporation and complaining about some of the problems within the Human Resources department. Jack was embarrassed and thought it was very unprofessional to trash the company in front of someone outside the company. Jack's apologies were accepted, but he was sure that they made a lasting impression with the vendor about what type of company they were to do business with.

LESSON LEARNED
Minimize unprofessionalism by setting the ground rules for the project team at the beginning of the project.

The project team members are given the responsibility of representing their organization in the technology acquisition. In order to represent their organization adequately, it is essential that they be considered the most knowledgeable people in their organization. Make sure that your team members are seasoned and considered experts within their competency. This will ensure that the organization's requirements are represented and prioritized correctly in the decision-making process.

The last trait to look for in project team members is being easy to get along with. You will be spending days cooped up in conference rooms with these people for several months. Although it is not critical that you get along with team members, it will enable you to focus on the task at hand and not have to deal with challenging personalities.

Take the time to interview the project team members individually to ensure that they will enhance and not hinder the technology acquisition process. You, and your company, will be relying on these people in order to be successful.

Undesirable Project Team Members

Characteristics of incompetent project team members have the opposite character traits of those described previously. Watch out for project team members who are unreliable, unmotivated, untrustworthy, or who lack integrity.

If you can't rely on certain project team members, you will constantly be checking on them to make sure that they complete their tasks, show up on time, and are prepared. This will take your attention away from managing the project effectively. Make sure you have team members who you can count on to get the job done.

You are not a cheerleader. Your job is not to motivate the project team to try hard. Because of the critical nature of the decision that your project team is faced with, you want the best people in the organization on the project team. They should be able to motivate themselves. They have an enormous opportunity for exposure on the project and a great responsibility to their companies and their peers. If they don't want to seize this opportunity, find others who do.

Can you trust the project team member? This is difficult to judge if you don't have any background with a particular person. Ask around and find out what other managers who work with this person think of his or her trustworthiness. This person will have the ability to impact the final decision. Don't hand out this privilege to someone who has a poor track record.

Last, and most important in choosing team members, determine if they have integrity. If you can count on members to be honest and do the right thing, they will put what is right for the company before what is right for them.

Now that you have a list of character traits, those to look for and those to look out for, to help you select your project team members, make sure you do a thorough job in identifying the right people for your project team. Trust me, it will pay dividends in the long run when your project is a smashing success.

Securing Resources

There are two different methods for securing resources for your project team. You can either let the manager of each stakeholder business organization select his representative, or you can go out and recruit him yourself.

The value of having the manager of the stakeholder organization select a representative is obvious. A manager knows who his best resources are and who can represent his business effectively. At the same time, some managers might give you a poor resource because they want to keep their best people close to them where their benefits are most visible.

One way to resolve this problem is to meet with the managers of the stakeholder organizations and review your business case and project charter. Help them understand the importance of the acquisition and how it will improve their companies. If they know that there will be a significant impact to their operations, they will allocate a better resource to your team. If the impact is not significant, they are right to not give you their best resource.

Once you have identified your resources, have interviewed them, and are ready to move forward, take the time to meet with their direct managers. The goal of these meetings is to secure a percentage of your resources' time. If you don't do this early in the process, you might end up with resources being pulled away from your project. Be sure to get a time commitment from each of them up front to minimize the risk of losing valuable resource time.

Defining Reporting Relationships and Authority

While meeting with the team members' direct managers, define the reporting relationship and authority over them. Your best case is to have your resources report to you directly 100 percent of the time during the technology acquisition. However, as you probably know, this is an unlikely scenario. There is a lot of downtime during a technology acquisition. There will be times when you are waiting for a vendor, and there is no work to be done. For this reason, it is best to get 50 percent of your resources' time.

Once you have a commitment from their direct managers for 50 percent of their time, discuss the type of work team members will be doing on your project and what you expect of them. Also, ask if you can contribute to their annual review. If you are using them for 50 percent of their time for six months, you should try to get 25 percent of their annual review allocated to you. Project team members are sometimes reluctant to spend time away from their business organizations because they feel that their direct managers will not have any exposure to their work and, as a result, will bypass them for new opportunities or promotions. If you have a percentage of their review, they will be more willing to participate and put in more effort.

Defining and Communicating Performance Expectations

Once you have identified your resources, have secured their time, and have established their reporting relationships, it's time to define and communicate performance expectations. It is difficult for people to read your mind so do your best to capture your expectations of them on paper at the beginning of the project. Define the work to be completed, the amount of time that you expect them to complete it in, and the manner in which you expect them to conduct themselves. For example, you might state that you expect them to clearly define and prioritize their organization's functional requirements of the technology within the next two weeks, and you expect them to be on time to all meetings.

Resource Development Planning

A technology acquisition is a great opportunity for team members to gain exposure and become more educated in the process. When meeting with their direct managers, find out what their current career path is. Also, ask the person directly during your initial meetings. This will help you identify opportunities to develop your team members while they are contributing to the objectives of the project.

Let's suppose that one of your project team resources is pursuing a management opportunity within his organization. You might provide this person with the opportunity to display his management skills to his organization by getting him assigned as the person to implement the technology within his organization after the technology acquisition is complete. This will create a win-win situation for you and the team member. He will be more committed to the project if he knows that it will lead to an opportunity to display his management capabilities to his organization.

Defining a resource development plan is good for the company, good for the team member, and good for your project. Take the time to consider how you can develop your resources during the technology acquisition project.

It is not a bad idea to give your project team members a grace period to evaluate the project and determine if they want to be on the team. Express the importance of getting their commitment to stay on the team for the duration of the project. It can be a major setback to have an SME, representing a key stakeholder, leave the team late in the Research phase. Because you can't go back and start over, a new person will not be in a position to pick up where the other left off. Make sure you have a commitment from both the person and his direct manager to stay with the project before you start the Research phase.

The Project Kick-Off

The project kick-off meeting is very important to the success of the technology acquisition project. This is the first opportunity for the project team members to come together and learn about the initiative that they are about to participate in. You need to sell the importance of the project to the team in this meeting. One very effective way to accomplish this is to have the project sponsor and someone from the executive management team present their vision of the project's end result. This will let the project team members know how important the project is and help them understand the driving forces behind the effort. The following items should be part of the agenda for the project kick-off meeting:

- *Introductions:* Introduce all meeting attendees and summarize the purpose and agenda for the meeting.

- *Summary of business need:* Provide an overview of the business need that initiated the project. Make sure all questions are answered before continuing with the solution.

- *Summary of the solution:* Provide an overview of the solution that is proposed to address the business need.

- *Review of the project charter:* Provide an overview of the project charter.

- *Project sponsor presentation:* Have the project sponsor introduce himself. He should then proceed to communicate the vision for the project and what it means to the company. Although this might be repetitive of the previous agenda items, the project team needs to hear this information from the management team. This will reinforce the need and increase the perceived importance of the project in the project team's mind.

- *Executive management presentation:* Have executive management present the project as well. Although this is not required, it can be a bonus in conveying the importance of the project to the team members.

A polished and prepared project kick-off meeting will start the project off in the right direction and set a precedence of high standards for the effort.

3

Research

Initiation → Planning → **Research** → Evaluation → Negotiation → Implementation → Operation

The objective of the Research phase is to determine which vendor is best suited to address your business need. There are many research methods that can be used to become more educated about vendors and their technology.

This chapter provides an overview of nine potential research methods that can be used in your technology acquisition process.

The vendor sales team is also discussed in this chapter. During the technology acquisition process, you will be working with several vendor representatives. Gaining a better understanding of their role in the process will help you manage the vendor-customer relationship effectively.

THE RESEARCH PROCESS

The Research process consists of nine potential subprocesses (for example, research methods): external research, external assessment, request for proposal (RFP), vendor site demo, vendor on-site demo, vendor reference calls, vendor customer site visit, vendor conference, and benchmark/pilot (Figure 3-1).

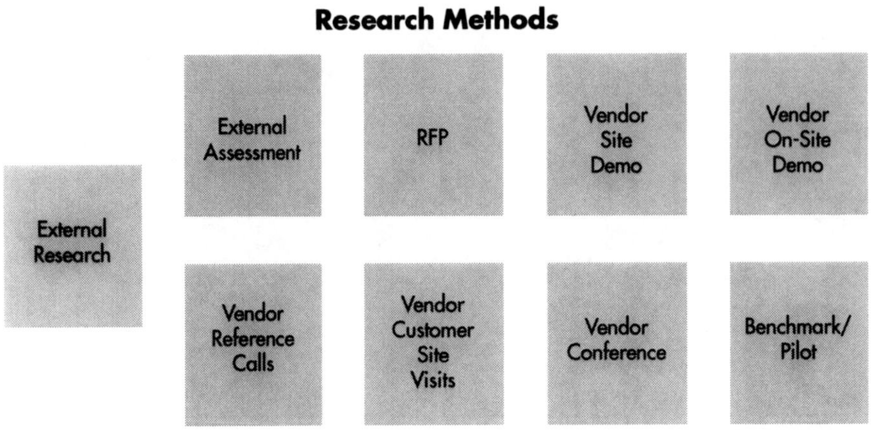

Research Methods

External Research

External Assessment

RFP

Vendor Site Demo

Vendor On-Site Demo

Vendor Reference Calls

Vendor Customer Site Visits

Vendor Conference

Benchmark/ Pilot

Figure 3-1: Research subprocesses

At the beginning of the Research phase, it is a good idea to meet with your project team members to explain what is expected of them regarding confidentiality.

Project team members must understand the confidential nature of the information that they will be exposed to. They should understand what a non-disclosure agreement (NDA) is and what it means to each company. Make sure you stress that they should honor these agreements by not sharing information about one vendor with another. Vendors will most likely be showing you their newest products, which are not yet available to the general public. Their competitors would love to know what they are working on. For this reason, many vendor representatives will ask questions about the other vendors. Instruct your project team members to remind the vendor that they are not at liberty to discuss another vendor due to the NDAs that were signed. Project team members should also be careful about how they ask questions of the vendors. For example, if vendor A's product supports the XYZ communication method, you shouldn't ask vendor B if its product supports the XYZ communication method. Instead, ask other vendors which communication methods they support. This type of question will give you the same answer without focusing on one specific answer. The exception to using this type of questioning is when you are communicating the same questions fairly to all vendors, for example, in an RFP.

You should also discuss keeping an open mind with your project team members. Suggest that they don't try to make a decision on which vendor they like best until after all research is complete and the Evaluation phase begins. This is very difficult because the natural tendency is to immediately start figuring out who the vendor favorite is. Many times project team members have said that they like one vendor over another halfway through the Research phase and end up changing their minds by the end of the Evaluation phase. Request that they remain as objective as possible and try not to share their opinion of which vendor is best until the Evaluation phase.

Discuss your expectations for social occasions involving vendors. For example, relate your policy on consuming alcoholic beverages when dining with vendors. If you allow project team members to consume alcoholic beverages, it might be a good idea to request that they limit their intake. People tend to act unprofessionally and talk more loosely when they have had a lot to drink. As discussed previously, the best policy is not to meet socially with vendors until after contracts are signed.

The nine methods that can be used to research vendors are listed in Table 3-1 along with the benefits and drawbacks of each method. You should use methods that allow a fair comparison of the vendors and their technology.

Table 3-1: Research Method Benefits versus Drawbacks

Research Method	Benefits	Drawbacks	Cost	Estimated Time
External Research	Low cost Timeline Objective evaluation Knowledge and experience	Dependence on integrity of researcher Lack of interface with vendors Dependence on thoroughness of researcher Timeliness of researcher Lack of confidential information	Low	1 week
External Assessment	Objective evaluation Knowledge and experience	Dependence on integrity of researcher Dependence on thoroughness of researcher Time Cost	High	2–4 weeks
RFP	Consistency Commitment Formalization Education Documentation Objectiveness	Your company's time and money Prospective vendor's time and money Prospective vendor's legal risk	Medium	4–5 weeks

(continued)

Table 3-1: Research Method Benefits versus Drawbacks (cont.)

Research Method	Benefits	Drawbacks	Cost	Estimated Time
Vendor Site Demo	Seeing the product Evaluate the vendor Importance of your business Evaluate the vendor's support capabilities Evaluate the vendor's technical knowledge	High costs Less control Scheduling challenges	High	2–3 weeks
Vendor On-site Demo	Seeing the product Greater involvement Vendor education Low cost Timeline Importance of your business	Scheduling challenges Less control Vendor costs	Low	1 week
Vendor Reference Calls	Low cost Timeline Vendor customer satisfaction Vendor integrity Experience Decisions Differences Contacts	Objectivity	Low	1 week
Vendor Customer Site Visit	Seeing the product New ideas Vendor customer satisfaction Vendor integrity Experience Decisions Differences Contacts	Time Cost Objectivity	High	2–3 weeks
Vendor Conference	Timeline Competition Comparison Cost Greater involvement Seeing the product	Scheduling challenges Less control Vendor costs	Medium	1 week

Research Method	Benefits	Drawbacks	Cost	Estimated Time
	Vendor education Importance of your business			
Benchmark/ Pilot	Proof of concept Proof of performance and scalability Proof of technology Seeing the product Test your environment Experience	Time Cost Scheduling challenges Vendor costs	High	1–2 weeks

Each research method is described in detail in the following sections. Assuming that you will use this book as a reference in the future to access just the research methods that you plan to use in your technology acquisition project, the same description for many of the benefits and drawbacks are intentionally repeated to ensure that they are complete.

External Research

The external research method involves purchasing research and expert advice from external resources. If you used an external resource for defining your solution (see Chapter 2), you may be able to leverage the same source.

There are several companies that objectively evaluate industries, trends, markets, technologies, and businesses. Some of these companies publish reports and sell them. This option allows you to leverage another company's expertise in the industry. If the technology you are acquiring is new to your organization, you might not know which questions to ask when evaluating vendors and their technologies. If this is the case, it might be wise to purchase research from a company that specializes in understanding and evaluating the technology you are acquiring.

The external research method can be very effective. The following list provides an overview of the benefits in using this research method:

Low cost: Obtaining research from external sources can be inexpensive or even free. In some cases, the research can be somewhat expensive. In either case, the cost may be less than what it would cost you to conduct the research yourself.

Timeline: Researching vendors can be very time-consuming. For example, using the RFP research method can take weeks to develop and a month for vendors to respond with a proposal. Add a few weeks to evaluate vendor proposals, and you're up to two months. Vendor conferences, benchmarks/pilots, and vendor customer site visits can also be very time intensive. If you are in a big hurry to select a vendor, the fastest research method is to purchase the necessary information from a company that specializes in researching the technology that you are acquiring.

Objective evaluation: A third-party research company will provide an objective evaluation of the vendors and their technologies. Although it is possible that a research company could favor a vendor unfairly, the research company's integrity and reputation will suffer as a result. If you select a solid company with a reputation for quality and integrity to supply the research, you will receive very objective and thorough research information.

Knowledge and experience: If you can find a research company that specializes in the technology that you are acquiring, you will benefit from its knowledge and experience. The company will know the history of the industry, have experience with the technology, and know what questions to ask in order to differentiate the vendors. In some cases, a consulting company with experience implementing the technology can be a good source of external research.

There are also a number of drawbacks to using the external research method. The following list discusses a few of these drawbacks:

Dependency on integrity of researcher: One of the challenges of managing a technology acquisition project is maintaining objectivity throughout the process. When you opt to purchase your research, you are relying on the researcher to provide you with an objective analysis. You must determine how important this technology is to your company and whether you can afford to take this risk. If you do decide to use an outside researcher, it might be wise to validate some of the research to ensure its quality.

Lack of interface with vendors: The relationships established with the vendors during the technology acquisition process can be very beneficial in the long term. You need the vendors to understand your business and you need to understand theirs in order for the relationship to be mutually beneficial. Buying the research does not require interfacing with the vendors, which is critical in building a solid working relationship with your vendors.

Dependency on thoroughness of researcher: How thorough is the research? Can you guarantee that the researchers have uncovered all of the essential information? You have no way of knowing the answers to these questions if you buy the research instead of conducting it yourself. Although external research can be very beneficial, it's a risky proposition to rely only on this method.

Timeliness of research: When was the last time the research company updated its information? Keep in mind that the research you receive may not be current. With technology reinventing itself at such a rapid pace, the already outdated information could be obsolete in six months. If you do purchase research, make sure you understand when it was collected.

Lack of confidential information: Confidential information cannot be shared. Because researchers are in the business of sharing information for a fee, how can they expect to receive confidential information from the vendors? They can't. Conducting your own research, with an NDA in effect, ensures that you will receive confidential information about products that are still in design and development. It is very important to know where the vendor is going with its technology. For this reason, it might not be wise to rely solely on external researchers for your information.

TIPS

✔ Find out which method researchers use to evaluate markets, vendors, and technologies. This will help you determine the quality of the information that they will provide.

✔ Check references for the researchers to ensure that they deliver the quality that they say they will deliver.

✔ Beware of alliances or any other type of relationships between the researchers and the vendors. This could influence the research significantly in favor of one vendor.

External Assessment

A third-party company can be hired to conduct an assessment of the vendor to evaluate the vendor's capabilities. There are several models that can be used to measure vendor capabilities fairly and objectively. The Software Engineering Institute (SEI) publishes a model called the Capability Maturity Model (CMM). This model measures the vendor's ability to use repeatable processes across its organization. Another model that is commonly used in evaluating a company's use of standards is the International Organization for Standardization (ISO) standard. Regardless of which model is used, it can be very beneficial to have a third-party company evaluate the vendor's organization and its capabilities.

There are several benefits in using the external assessment research method. The following list provides an overview of these benefits:

Objective evaluation: A third-party research company will provide an objective evaluation of a vendor's capabilities. Although it is possible that a research company could favor a vendor unfairly, the research company's integrity and reputation will suffer as a result. If you select a solid company with a reputation for quality and integrity to conduct the evaluation, you will receive a very objective and thorough vendor capability assessment.

Knowledge and experience: If you can find a research company that specializes in the technology that you are acquiring, you will benefit from its knowledge and experience. The company will know the history of the industry, have experience with the technology, and know which questions to ask in order to assess a vendor's capabilities.

There are also a number of drawbacks to using the external assessment research method. The following list discusses a few of these drawbacks:

Dependency on integrity of researcher: One of the challenges of managing a technology acquisition project is maintaining objectivity throughout the process. When you contract with an external researcher, you are relying on the researcher to provide you with an objective analysis.

Dependency on thoroughness of researcher: How thorough is the third-party company's evaluation methodology? Can you be sure that you are getting feedback on the right differences in functionality, technology, and strategic partnership potential? Ask for examples of the research company's work and check references if necessary.

Time: It can take a considerable amount of time for a company to assess each of the vendor's operations and conduct a thorough evaluation of the vendor's entire operation.

Cost: This research method can be very costly as you will be hiring a third-party to send several of its employees to each of the vendor's sites and spend several weeks evaluating the vendor's operations.

TIPS

✔ Take the time to gain an understanding of the different models used by a third-party research company to assess vendor capabilities. This is the only way to ensure that the company is evaluating the criteria that are important to you in a vendor.

✔ Find out if the vendor has already had a third-party company conduct a capability assessment. If the assessment was recent enough, you may be able to hire the same third-party researcher to only evaluate the other vendors using the same model and criteria. This can save you the cost of assessing at least one of the vendors.

RFP

The RFP is a tool used to thoroughly research and evaluate vendors. It clearly documents the buyer's functionality, technology, strategic partnership potential, and cost requirements for the prospective vendors. At the same time, it requests that the vendor's response be in a predefined format. This provides you with a fair and objective comparison of each vendor and streamlines the Evaluation phase. An RFP also tells you a lot about the prospective vendors, such as how thorough they are and how much they value your business. A sloppy RFP, chock-full of standard literature, is a clear indicator that the vendor didn't feel that your business was worth a considerable effort on its part.

There are several benefits to using the RFP research method. The following list provides an overview of these benefits:

Consistency: RFPs provide a consistent avenue for researching prospective vendors. All vendors receive the same document with the same list of requirements. Prospective vendors will be more likely to dedicate time and resources to winning the contract if they know they will have a fair chance to compete for your business.

Commitment: By clearly documenting what you are asking for and having the vendor clearly document what it is committing to provide, you will be more likely to receive what you asked for and be able to build a successful relationship with clear expectations on both sides. In the case where a vendor misrepresents the truth about its company or product's capabilities, you will be in a better position to negotiate a resolution with the vendor or take legal action.

Formalization: By documenting your requirements and how you want prospective vendors to respond to those requirements in an RFP, you formalize the process of researching the vendors. This will also streamline the Evaluation phase.

Education: An RFP provides a great way to become educated about the market, vendors, and technologies available. This is particularly helpful if it is the first implementation of this particular technology within your company.

Clarity: The process of creating an RFP forces you to define your requirements in more detail. This helps you and the vendor gain a better understanding of the requirements.

Documentation: RFPs help you document the decision process. This can be extremely helpful when objections arise within your organization. In a previous acquisition, I had involved several people from the Management Information Systems (MIS) department on the project. Everything was moving forward on schedule until an MIS Director who hadn't been aware of the effort tried to put the brakes on the project. I was able to provide him with thorough documentation outlining everything that had been done and who was involved. That was all it took to eliminate that obstacle. You may also run into a situation where a new manager joins your company who has used a different vendor at his previous company. This documentation will help him understand why the vendor of choice is the right vendor for your company's needs.

Objectiveness: The proposals will help you rate the vendors fairly and arrive at an objective decision. You may not always decide on using the vendor with the highest scores, but this information will provide you with a better understanding of the decision you are making.

There are also a number of drawbacks to using the RFP research method. The following list discusses a few of these drawbacks:

Your company's time and money: A formal RFP takes time and resources from your organization to create. It also takes a considerable amount of time to review all of the proposals. Project managers need to weigh this disadvantage when deciding which research methods to incorporate into their Research phase.

Prospective vendor's time and money: You may have vendors decline to respond to your RFP. Usually they will wait to see the RFP first and then decide whether they want to participate further. Vendors need to decide whether they are likely to win the deal, whether they have the resources available to respond effectively, and whether they have the resources or technology to meet your requirements. If any of these criteria cannot be met, they might not be able to justify the time and expense of participating in the process. In the past, I've had vendors that were superior to their competitors decline participation due to limited resources.

Prospective vendor's legal risk: Some vendors don't want to take the risk of committing to what they will provide in writing. This gives the buyer the ability to take legal action more effectively if the vendor cannot live up to its claims.

See the RFP sample and template for more information.

TIPS

✔ Be very specific about the types of references you would like from the vendor. You can specify this in the RFP if you are using that research method. The more similar the reference is to your organization, the more relevant the information will be that you receive from them. If you are a very large organization, you wouldn't want a small startup company as a reference. On the flip side, if you are a very small startup company, you wouldn't want a very large company as a reference. Both types of organizations have very different business models, needs, and challenges.

✔ Have all project team members who are involved in the strategic partnership evaluation attend the vendor reference calls. It is important that you have the project team members attend all or none of the vendor reference calls; otherwise, you are not fairly evaluating vendors. If you must divide the work, assign one reference for each vendor to a project team member. This will still allow members to be fair and evaluate all vendors equally.

✔ Try to call at least three references for each vendor. This will allow you to compare notes to see what trends emerge.

✔ You might want to ask vendors to provide a list of questions that they recommend be included in the RFP. This will help define the questions your company should be asking in its RFP. In my experience, the result of using this approach was that each vendor asked the questions that illustrated the good points about its solution and the bad points of its competitor's solution. Compiling all vendors' questions into one list allows you to draw out the good and bad of all the vendors' solutions. Additionally, this technique can educate you about the technology by helping you to understand the key differences between vendors. If you are acquiring a technology for the first time and have limited knowledge of the technology, this can be very helpful to your project team.

Template

REQUEST FOR PROPOSAL

LETTER OF INTENT
Sent from the project sponsor to the vendor's management team, this letter summarizes the objectives of the project and requests the management team's participation in the technology acquisition process.

TABLE OF CONTENTS
Provides an outline of the contents of the document.

GENERAL INFORMATION
Provides the vendor with general information about the technology acquisition. Examples include purpose of the RFP, where to direct communications regarding the RFP, timetable for the process, statements about who will be responsible for RFP response costs, number of proposals required, requirements for effective dates of pricing, overview of the criteria for the decision-making process, a statement about your company's right to reject proposals, and a statement requiring written permission to use your company's name in any marketing material.

VENDOR GUIDELINES AND REQUIRED PROPOSAL FORMAT
Describes the guidelines for how you would like the vendors to structure their proposals. The more consistent the proposal formats are, the easier it is to compare vendors fairly.

PRODUCT OVERVIEW
Requests that the vendor provide an overview of its product offerings (marketing materials) in this section of the proposal.

FUNCTIONALITY
Lists all functionality requirements for the new solution. It is also beneficial to include a list of response codes and the corresponding descriptions at the beginning of this section. Include a column for the vendor to fill in the appropriate code for each requirement (see the following sample RFP). The following table can be used as a template for the functionality requirements.

#	Requirement	Code	Response
1	<Requirement>	<code>	<open for vendor's response>
2	<Requirement>	<code>	<open for vendor's response>
3	<Requirement>	<code>	<open for vendor's response>
4	<Requirement>	<code>	<open for vendor's response>
5	<Requirement>	<code>	<open for vendor's response>

TECHNOLOGY

Lists all technology requirements for the new solution. There may also be questions about the vendor's solution technology. The following table can be used as a template for the technology requirements.

#	Requirement	Response
1	<Requirement>	<open for vendor's response>
2	<Requirement>	<open for vendor's response>
3	<Requirement>	<open for vendor's response>
4	<Requirement>	<open for vendor's response>
5	<Requirement>	<open for vendor's response>

STRATEGIC PARTNERSHIP POTENTIAL

Lists questions to determine how well the vendor meets your requirements as a strategic technology partner. Questions can address the vendor profile, training, support, vendor experience, vendor's typical implementation plan, vendor's technology leadership ability, and customer reference criteria.

COST

Lists questions to determine the short- and long-term costs associated with the new solution.

APPENDIX

Used to attach informational items, such as company information, information about your company's computing environment, and/or your company's standard terms of agreement (contracts).

Due to the criticality of the RFP document, I have included a sample RFP that was used in a successful technology acquisition. The names have been changed to protect the involved parties.

SAMPLE RFP

XYZ Corporation

REQUEST FOR PROPOSAL

March 2001

SAMPLE RFP

January 1, 2001

LETTER OF TRANSMITTAL

Dear Prospective Vendors,
XYZ Corporation (XYZ), the leading calculator manufacturer, is in the process of selecting a strategic vendor to partner with XYZ in providing the optimal customer experience through the application of workforce management technology within our call centers. We feel the opportunity exists to leverage the depth and breadth of delivery solutions available through strategic vendors, allowing us to focus on our core competencies and meet our corporate mission. A significant component of the overall solution is the need for managing our resources effectively.

XYZ supports its customers via a number of delivery options: traditional phone support, Internet and online services, letters and faxes, automated attendant/troubleshooting systems, FaxBack systems, and mail-in service. Customer Support is segmented in the following manner: General Technical Support (supporting individuals, families, enthusiasts, small business, and education customers), Major Accounts Support (for large, corporate customers and government agencies), International Support (customers owning XYZ calculators in international regions not covered by XYZ international sites), and Customer Service (nontechnical support such as order status, cancellations, refunds, etc.). Each of these groups has its own forecast and requires workforce scheduling.

XYZ uses the services of several outsource call centers to enhance its availability to its customers. We currently provide a monthly and interval forecast to each outsource center, which in turn does its own scheduling. The strategic plan calls for a ramp-down in the percentage of calls XYZ outsources. Outsource companies currently handle (30%) of XYZ's overall support volumes. Our internal support is currently spread across 12 U.S. sites, and we will add 4 more by years' end.

XYZ is currently handling approximately 16,000 calls per day, distributed as follows in each of the following segments: General: (10,000 total, and 7,000 internal versus 3,000 external, AHT = 15 min.) Major Accounts: (1,500 internal, AHT = 11 min.) International: (500 internal, AHT = 12 min.) Customer Service: (4,000 internal, AHT = 3 min.)

We expect that volume to increase by (35%) in the next 12 months.

XYZ routes its calls in the following manner: Customers call 800 numbers and choose options from a conversant. Using XXX Intelligent Call Router, calls are distributed to the center, which real-time calculation suggests will have the shortest answer time. Some calls are still routed using percent allocation from an AAA platform.

As we move into the future, we intend to move as much volume as possible to our automated options such as the Internet. It is important to XYZ to be able to model various scenarios to help us plan and schedule for this strategy, and show the effects on the current phone workforce in terms of headcount numbers and staff schedules. We also expect to bring up 6–10 additional support centers in the next 24 months.

There are two more initiatives that demand attention for support. First, we will launch an initiative to further segment our support volumes to facilitate both internal productivity and the optimal customer experience. This will require extensive modeling (given the fact that we're a multisite environment layered with several customer segments and business segments). Second, we plan to implement some "down-the-wire" support strategies to aid productivity and call resolution rates.

The workforce management technology is anticipated to provide XYZ with the following:

- Improved productivity
- Improved information for management decisions
- Improved efficiency
- Flexible processing environments/architectures
- Vendor assisted technology transitions and solutions
- Vendor value-added differentiation
- Strategic partnership with a leading edge workforce management vendor

This RFP is meant to define and document our functional needs and also establish a consistent basis on which workforce management vendor proposals can be judged. XYZ and/or its designees will evaluate all proposals.

This RFP and all materials submitted by XYZ are to be treated as strictly confidential. As a prospective workforce management vendor, you must not forward any such materials or

(continued)

SAMPLE RFP (*cont.*)

otherwise disclose their content to any third party for evaluation or for any other purpose without XYZ's written consent.

Please carefully review the guidelines for Proposals established in the RFP. Your proposal should describe in detail your application's functionality, technological merit, competitive costing, ease of use, technical assistance plans as well as specify all associated costs. Prospective workforce management vendors should develop and present their costs with the intention that it represents the "last, final, and best" price. Your ability to meet clearly and precisely the needs outlined in the RFP will directly impact our evaluation process. XYZ reserves the right to modify the general scope of the RFP prior to proposal submission.

Vendors who apply creativity and flexibility, along with their resident in-house knowledge and expertise, will enhance the consideration their proposal receives. Multiple solution scenarios or variations on a theme may be offered. The requirements outlined in Sections I and II must be met.

For informational purposes, this RFP and your proposal will also be provided to XXX, Real-life Consulting, and General Service Networking.

We appreciate your consideration and assistance in this matter and look forward to receiving your proposal.

Sincerely,

Dave Johnson
VP of Information Technology
XYZ Corporation

SAMPLE RFP

1   General Information
1.1   Purpose of the RFP
1.2   RFP Communications
1.3   Timeline
1.4   RFP Preparation
1.5   Vendor Responses
1.6   Effective Dates of Pricing
1.7   Vendor Site Visits
1.8   Evaluation Criteria
1.9   Right to Reject
1.10 Marketing References

2   Vendor Guidelines
2.1   RFP Response Format
2.2   Exceptions to the RFP
2.3   Confidentiality

3   Product Information

4   Functionality Requirements
4.1   Forecasting
4.2   Scheduling
4.3   Reporting
4.4   Real-Time Adherence

5   Technology Requirements
5.1   Client
5.2   Network Architecture, Scalability, Extensibility
5.3   Integration

6   Strategic Partnership Potential
6.1   Vendor Profile
6.2   Training
6.3   Support
6.4   Experience
6.5   Implementation Plan
6.6   Thought Leadership
6.7   References

7   Costs
7.1   Initial Costs
7.2   Long-Term Costs
7.3   Payment Options

(continued)

SAMPLE RFP (*cont.*)

1   General Information
1.1   Purpose of the RFP

The purpose of the Request for Proposal (RFP) is to establish the functional, operational, and technical requirements for the procurement of a workforce management system that best meets XYZ's requirements.

1.2   RFP Communications

Please direct all communications/correspondence regarding this RFP to:

Mike Smith
XYZ
610 XYZ Dr., S-22
Anywhere, WA 98134-2000
(206) 555-2042 x134
(206) 555-1161 (FAX)

Prospective workforce management vendors failing to observe this policy may be eliminated from the final evaluation.

1.3   Timeline

Vendor demo, review, and site visit	August
RFP submission date	August 8
Proposal due date	August 26
Vendor selection and contracts	August 26–September

1.4   RFP Preparation

The prospective vendors will absorb all costs incurred in the preparation and presentation of an RFP. In the event that modifications or additions to the RFP become necessary, prospective vendors will be notified in writing. All supporting materials submitted with the proposal will become the property of XYZ unless otherwise requested by the prospective vendors at time of submission.

1.5   Vendor Responses

Prospective vendors are required to submit six (6) copies of their proposals. Send all copies to Mike Smith no later than August 26, 1997. All supporting materials and documentation must be included with the proposal.

1.6 Effective Dates of Pricing

Prospective vendors should state in writing that all furnished information, including pricing, will remain valid and applicable for a minimum of one hundred twenty (120) days from the date their proposal is received by XYZ.

1.7 Vendor Site Visits

XYZ reserves the right to inspect any and all vendor facilities, which will be used to support the proposed workforce management solution. This includes the facilities of any contractor or outside support organization that will be used.

1.8 Evaluation Criteria

Prospective vendor proposals will be evaluated using the following general criteria:
- Ability to satisfy functional business requirements
- Ability to satisfy technical and integration requirements
- Strategic partnering potential
- Cost

1.9 Right to Reject

XYZ reserves the right to accept or reject any and/or all submitted proposals and request additional information from all prospective vendors. XYZ specifically reserves the right to negotiate a contract with the selected vendor(s). The vendor's response to this RFP will be included in whole or by reference in the final contract. At the discretion of XYZ, a third-party financial institution or consulting team could be included in contract negotiations. Any contract that is eventually awarded will be made to the organization who, based on the evaluation of all responses, applying all criteria and oral interviews (if required), is determined to be the best qualified to provide the requested solution and support.

1.10 Marketing References

Prospective vendors may not make any reference to the project in any literature, promotional material, brochures or sales presentations, or make any other commercial use of XYZ's name and/or this RFP, without the express written consent of XYZ. However, XYZ will offer itself as a reference account to the selected vendor(s).

Copyrights used herein are acknowledged to be the property of their prospective companies.

(continued)

SAMPLE RFP (*cont.*)

2   Vendor Guidelines

2.1   RFP Response Format

Prospective vendors should make every attempt to use terminology in their proposal that is consistent with that of XYZ and this RFP. Comparable terminology may be substituted, where appropriate, if the prospective vendor provides clear and concise definitions. Prospective vendor proposals should address the requirements outlined in this RFP as directly and concisely as possible. Extraneous information with no apparent connection to XYZ and this RFP could detract from the proposal scoring.

The information furnished should be in specific response to this RFP. Specific answers are required to specific questions where asked. Supplemental information should be prepared on standard 8½ × 11 inch paper.

Vendor responses to this RFP will become a part of the final contract between XYZ and the vendor.

Prospective vendors are requested to provide their proposal in the following format:

Letter of Transmittal

The letter of transmittal should be no longer than two (2) pages and should include the following:
- A brief statement of the vendor's understanding of the mission-critical nature of the workforce management technology to XYZ's business and market position.
- A brief statement of the services to be provided.
- A statement of commitment to provide the services requested within the time and manner specified.
- The names of personnel authorized to represent the vendor, including titles, addresses, phone and FAX numbers. XYZ would prefer to deal with a single representative.
- A summary of the prospective vendor's qualifications to perform this type of engagement.

Table of Contents

The table of contents should include a clear and complete identification of the materials submitted by section and page number.

Product Overview

Prospective vendors should follow the instructions in the Product Overview section of this RFP.

Functional Requirements

Prospective vendors should follow the instructions in the Functional Product Information section of this RFP.

Technical Requirements

Prospective vendors should respond to all technical information requests in the Technical Product Information section of this RFP.

Strategic Partnership Potential

Prospective vendors should provide the information requested in the Strategic Partnership Potential section of this RFP.

Cost Requirements

Prospective vendors should provide the information requested in the Cost Summary section of this RFP.

Appendix

Prospective vendors may provide any other information that the vendor considers appropriate for this proposal in an Appendix.

2.2 Exceptions to the RFP

Prospective vendors may find instances where their operations do not function in a manner consistent with the specifications in the RFP. In such cases, it is permissible to take exception to portions of the RFP. The exceptions should be clearly identified. If necessary, attach an additional page describing the scope of the exceptions, any additional costs, and a summary of any advantages these exceptions represent to XYZ.

2.3 Confidentiality

This RFP and all materials submitted by XYZ must be considered confidential. XYZ requests that this RFP not be copied and not be forwarded to any third party for evaluation or for any other purpose without XYZ's express written consent. All prospective vendor personnel should note that they are under a signed, mutual confidentiality agreement.

When submitting confidential material to XYZ, prospective vendors must clearly mark it as such.

3   Product Information

Prospective vendors should include an overview of their total workforce management solution. Define each product offered by your organization and provide a brief description of its role in your total solution. Vendors may include screen examples and/or diagrams in this section.

(continued)

SAMPLE RFP (*cont.*)

4   Functionality Requirements

4.1 Instructions

XYZ will be aggressive and comprehensive in its product/service demands. It is incumbent upon the vendor to provide measurable, accurate, and reliable answers based upon the vendor's proposed product solution specific to the dependencies of release level and features of both the vendor's and other vendor's products. When your product does not meet a requirement, a clear statement to that effect would be the most prudent approach. For each requirement, the solutions capability should be identified as follows:

NA   Not Available

MJ   Major Modification

This could be in the form of modifying the code of the product. This response will require an explanation specifying the amount of effort required in "person days."

MN   Minor Modification

Minor modifications include customization of a tool or report. Minor modifications should be demonstrable.

FR   Future Release

The requirement will be addressed in a forthcoming revision of the product. These responses require listing scheduled release dates in the explanation column.

CR   Current Release

The requirement is met in the current release and can be demonstrated.

TP   Third-Party Solution

The functional requirement is not offered by your company but can be seamlessly integrated into your package using a third party's product. The explanation should specify the third-party vendor and integration, and this function should be demonstrable where possible.

Requirements that are given a capability rating of MJ, MN, FR, or TP must have a brief description regarding how the requirement will be met. Those responses not answerable on the explanation area of the RFP should be identified by business area (e.g., Reporting) with the requirement's sequence number on a separate document. Vendors may add additional items or sections if there is functionality provided by their product that isn't represented in the following sections.

4.2 Forecasting

General Requirements

#	Requirement	Rating	Response
1	Forecast incoming calls		
2	Forecast outgoing calls		
3	Forecast incoming online requests		
4	Forecast incoming faxes		
5	Ability to forecast and track on a monthly, weekly (running 6-8 week forecast), daily, and intraday basis		
6	What methods does your system support for providing schedule, OT, vacation, and performance data to the agents?		

Forecasting Overall Demand

#	Requirement	Rating	Response
1	Forecast overall call demand including split/skills and callbacks		
2	Forecast overall incoming online request demand		
3	Forecast overall incoming fax demand		
4	Describe how your system accounts for holidays, nonoperational days, special days, and seasons in the forecast		

Forecasting Staffing Requirements

#	Requirement	Rating	Response
1	Forecast demand level: • With noncall demand • With only call demand • With available secondary skills • Without available secondary • With all or several sites • By site		
2	Forecast by skill: • For all sites • By site		

(continued)

SAMPLE RFP (*cont.*)

4.3 Scheduling
General Scheduling Requirements

#	Requirement	Rating	Response
1	Accommodate schedules that run over		
2	Accommodate different time zones		

Scheduling by Demand

#	Requirement	Rating	Response
1	Able to schedule and optimize staff to cover the following demand levels: • With noncall demand • With only call demand • With available secondary skills considered • Without available secondary skills considered • With all or several sites • By site		
2	Able to schedule and optimize staff to cover the following skill levels: • For all sites • By site • By team		
3	Schedule overall by: • Split/skill • Site • Team		
4	Track vacation time taken by each agent.		
5	How does the system assign vacation to agents without leaving the center or split/skill understaffed?		
6	Can the system determine which agents are willing to work OT and automatically assign if needed?		
7	Compare scheduled staff to forecast required staff by interval and distribute a required line to: • Each site based on schedules • Each team based on schedules		

Optimal Schedules

#	Requirement	Rating	Response
1	Create an optimum overall schedule (all sites combined)		
2	Create optimum schedules for each site		
3	Create optimum schedules by looking at available primary and secondary skills		

Scenarios

#	Requirement	Rating	Response
1	Create and save multiple what-if scenarios.		
2	Compare various scenarios		

Service Level Optimization

#	Requirement	Rating	Response
1	Optimize schedule through: • Break optimization • Schedule changes • Overtime assignment (The system must tell us the best time for OT and which teams/staff would be optimum.) • Addition/deletion of outsource vendor calls		
2	Real-time schedule adjustments from real-time data feeds from CMS (real-time link between WFM and CMS, Geotel, and Kronos) and suggest schedule modifications based on real-time situation automatically—more than just real-time adherence.		
3	Optimize service levels and show net effects on "required line net staffing" by providing best times for planned off-phone activities such as: • Training • Pre-approved vacation • Meetings • Other nonphone activities (e.g., incoming online requests, faxes, etc.)		

(continued)

SAMPLE RFP (*cont.*)

4.4 Reporting
Reporting Requirements

#	Requirement	Rating	Response
1	Report and optimize on an intraday basis because of unplanned changes in: • Demand • Net staffing • Service levels by site		
2	Provide original intraday forecast, revised forecast, and actual results comparisons		
3	Provide intraday schedule, demand, AHT, and off-phone time by: • Overall company • Site • Split/skill • Team		
4	Provide reporting via the intranet. What vendor (Netscape or Microsoft) and what version of output will the system support for creating HTML reports?		
5	Deliver real-time info to team manager's desktops by: • Team • Skill sets • Site • All sites		
6	Compare an agent's scheduled hours versus actual hours		
7	Compare actual hours to paid hours		
8	How does your system support moving agents between teams?		
9	How does your system obtain month-end results (via daily archives of the system or from month-end switch data)?		

4.5 Real-Time Adherence

Real-Time Adherence Requirements

#	Requirement	Rating	Response
1	Display comparisons of schedule information with ACD data for individuals on a real-time basis.		
2	Allow many simultaneous clients (35/site) to administer schedule exceptions reporting on a real-time basis.		

5 Technology Requirements
5.1 Client

#	Requirement	Response
1	Describe the minimum workstation requirements.	
2	List the operating system(s) supported by your system on the clients.	
3	Describe the method used by the client to communicate with your dialer?	
4	Is your client application 16 or 32 bit? If 16, when do you plan to support a 32-bit client?	
5	Does your application support API calls? If yes, please provide API documentation in the appendix.	
6	Does your application support DDE?	
7	Does your application support OLE? If yes, what version?	
8	Does your system use ODBC drivers on the client? If yes, which vendors and versions are supported?	
9	Can agents or administrators access the system remotely? If yes, which software or hardware is required to do so?	
10	List the total number of clients that can log into the system simultaneously.	
11	How does the total number of clients impact the system performance? How can this be improved?	

(continued)

SAMPLE RFP (*cont.*)

5.2 Network Architecture, Scalability, Extensibility
Scalability

#	Requirement	Response
1	Describe the smallest expandable system configuration possible with your system.	
2	Can system expansion be implemented easily? Please explain.	
3	Is the system, from a migration standpoint, compatible with previous versions of this product? Can your system migrate data from other vendor systems? If yes, which ones and describe the migration process.	
4	How many concurrent users and maximum users will your system support?	
5	Can your system support multiple locations? Please describe typical multisite implementations.	
6	Can your system support remote access? Describe the method in which this is accomplished.	

Architecture

#	Requirement	Response
1	Describe the technology base and architectural platform of the proposed system.	
2	Does your system employ true client/server technology? Please describe how this is accomplished.	
3	Describe how your system supports an open, standards-based architecture for all subsystems, components, hardware, software, and interfaces. Is there any proprietary hardware required for your system?	
4	If the system proposed by the vendor utilizes a distributed processing architecture, define the function of each processor as well as its relationship to all other processors.	
5	Does your system support TCP/IP as a network communications protocol? What vendors and what versions are supported?	
6	Explain your system's upload/download capabilities.	
7	What network operating systems are supported by your system? What NOS certifications does your company have?	
8	Define the planned enhancements and upgrades to the hardware platform for the next five years. Detailed plans are required for the next two years, with summary plans accepted for the remaining three years. Include migration path from the current products to the planned ones as part of your response.	

(continued)

SAMPLE RFP (*cont.*)

System Performance, Reliability, and Redundancy

#	Requirement	Response
1	Describe the design strategies that have been incorporated in your proposed system to ensure 24×7 availability.	
2	The vendor shall identify any routine or preventative maintenance activities that require the system to be less than fully available for normal operations. Describe the nature and extent of system outage required for these functions.	
3	The vendor must identify the average time required to completely initialize the system. This time shall be calculated to include the interval from command issuance until all system functionality has been restored.	
4	XYZ desires that the Call Center System be capable of recovery from a major outage with little or no impact to either its members or call center personnel. Describe any capabilities for load sharing between systems, hot standby systems, or other strategies that would significantly minimize the impact of a major system outage.	
5	For your five largest installed customers who have this proposed system hardware and software, indicate the number of seats supported and the maximum call volumes (both over LAN and WAN if available).	
6	What processes are the most time and resource intensive and why? Which processes affect performance when the maximum number of users are using the system and how do they affect performance?	
7	Describe how recoverable the proposed solution is if a power failure (post UPS failure) occurs on the workforce management system hardware platform; on the application server. Will the in-transit data be lost? Offer the likely scenarios and describe how the proposed solution will react to the failure.	
8	Can your system automatically send e-mails when a problem occurs using MS Outlook or MS Exchange Mail?	

Automated Execution

#	Requirement	Response
1	Does the application startup or shutdown require any operator replies? a) Explain the sequence of events that constitutes a startup. b) Explain the sequence of events that constitutes a shutdown.	
2	Can the system be "trained" to perform routine tasks in an unattended mode such as generating/printing reports?	

(continued)

SAMPLE RFP (*cont.*)

Data Flexibility

#	Requirement	Response
1	XYZ requires that the database provide unrestricted or unlimited use of the data elements provided by the system. Please provide a list of the data elements that are reported on.	
2	Can new columns be added to an existing table without having to change programs already accessing those tables?	
3	Can new columns be added dynamically, or must the data be unloaded and reloaded after the table definition has been changed?	
4	Are there limits to the file sizes and row sizes supported by your system?	
5	What DBMSs are supported by your system and what versions (specifically, Sybase system 11)? What are your DBMS plans for the future?	
6	What DBMS options are available or required with your system?	
7	How flexible and expandable is the DBMS? Can we add other data to the DBMS?	
8	Does the DBMS include any internal security mechanisms?	
9	Does the DBMS include distributed capabilities?	
10	Is your DBMS ODBC compliant?	
11	Does your system accommodate dates beyond the year 2000?	
12	Does the product include a complete set of utilities for managing the database? Please describe the user interface to these utilities.	
13	Is all of the data in your system stored in a DBMS? If so, which one(s)? If not, what other file structures are used to store data?	
14	What operating system(s) does the DBMS run under?	
15	Describe how your system supports/maintains data integrity.	

Communication & Connectivity

#	Requirement	Response
1	What is the minimum recommended local bandwidth for the product (i.e., 4 MB Token-Ring, 10 MB Ethernet, FDDI)? What is the optimum recommended bandwidth?	
2	Does the product require a specific transport (Ethernet, Token-Ring) to communicate to the desktop device? If so, which one(s)?	
3	What protocol(s) does the product use to communicate to the client workstation? Please list all that apply.	
4	Can the desktop (agent) workstations reside on a general population LAN, or is a separate network required? If so, what software is required?	
5	What is the maximum bandwidth available for downloading data from XYZ's server(s)? What is the recommended bandwidth?	
6	Can data updates be downloaded periodically, or must all information be downloaded at one time?	
7	WAN Connectivity: Local servers shall support router interface; indicate experience with various router protocols.	

Security

#	Requirement	Response
1	Describe the information security features of the product. a) How are user sign-ons controlled? b) How is access to programs, files, databases, objects, folders, etc., controlled? c) How is security administered? d) What are the audit features/capabilities?	
2	Networking between PCs must comply with a recognized and approved LAN. Describe how the system complies with this requirement.	
3	Multiple levels of security access are required for different functions, for example, unit manager can only access data for their group, administrator can update certain files but unit managers cannot, other users have "view only" capability. These security requirements apply to real-time and historical information.	

(continued)

SAMPLE RFP (*cont.*)

Software Recoverability

#	Requirement	Response
1	Does the system allow for daily unattended backup? a) Describe manual interventions required (if any). b) Does the system provide for host backup capability? c) Does the system allow for both full and incremental backups?	
2	What backup/restore techniques does your system support?	
3	Does the system provide for the automatic backup of magnetic disk for disaster recovery purposes?	
4	Does the vendor offer any special disaster recovery software?	
5	Is any proprietary hardware or software required? If yes, please identify.	
6	Identify potential environmental hazards to the system (e.g., static electricity, high humidity, temperature, etc.).	
7	Does the system automatically perform rollback processing during restart after a systemwide failure?	
8	Can the system provide for full recoverability in a 24×7 operating environment?	
9	Are there any remote site backup capabilities to be used for disaster recovery?	
10	Are UPS options and connectivity available with your system?	

Testing

#	Requirement	Response
1	Does your product offer application testing capability? What tools are available for testing of application changes?	
2	How are new, multiple, and test applications brought on-line in a system that is fully operational?	
3	Does your product have stress testing capability? How is this done? What is tested?	
4	Does your system provide any tools to facilitate testing? Please describe.	

5.3   Integration

#	Requirement	Response
1	*Internet/Intranet Integration* Describe how your system integrates with Internet/intranet technologies.	
2	*ACD Integration* What is your experience in integrating with Lucent G3R systems? How well do they integrate?	
3	*CMS Integration* What is your experience in integrating with CMS? How well do they integrate? Does the system support ANI collection?	
4	*Geotel Integration* What is your experience in integrating with Geotel? How well do they integrate?	
5	*MCI Integration* How does your system integrate with MCI data?	
6	*Chronus Integration* Does your system integrate with the Chronus time-clock system? How is this accomplished?	
7	*IVR Integration* How does your system use IVR technology? How does your system integrate with IVR systems?	
8	*Predictive Dialer Integration* How does your system integrate with predictive dialers? What predictive dialer systems does your system integrate with?	
9	*Client/Server Systems Integration* Describe how we might integrate our existing client/server applications with your system.	
10	*Imaging Integration* Describe your system's ability to integrate with imaging systems. Describe the typical method of integrating with imaging technology with your system.	
11	*Reporting Integration* What third-party reporting systems can use the data in your system?	
12	*Host Integration* Describe your system's ability to integrate with host systems. Describe the typical method of integrating host technology with your system. Does your system integrate with JDEdwards?	
13	*Client Software Integration* Will your system integrate with MS Office 97, MS Outlook, MS Schedule+, or MS Exchange Mail? If yes, please describe the method of integration.	

(continued)

SAMPLE RFP (*cont.*)

6   Strategic Partnership Potential
6.1 Vendor Profile
Prospective vendors must provide the following information:

- Describe your company's background and relationship to the workforce management industry. Please state historical dates, parent company if any, and mode of operation.
- Is this your company's only business? If no, please list other industries your company is involved with.
- What are your future plans in the workforce management arena?
- Provide annual reports and/or financial statements for the years 2000 and 2001. (Annual reports may be added to the Appendix). State timing of fiscal year end.
- List any special relationships with other companies that improve your ability to be a leader in the workforce management market.
- List any pertinent association memberships.
- Describe any legal issues or constraints that could conceivably affect a relationship with XYZ.

6.2 Training
Prospective vendors must provide the following information:

- Describe in detail your standard training program as well as installation assistance provided with your system.
- What system documentation is available and included in the price of the system?
- What additional training does your company offer?
- Do you have a certification process for your system? If yes, describe the process.

6.3 Support
Prospective vendors must provide the following information:

- Describe your system warranties.
- Describe maintenance plans available with your system.
- What are your response times?
- Describe the assistance that is available through your help desk, and during which hours it is available.
- Do you have a disaster recovery plan in place? Please describe.
- How frequently are preventive maintenance checks performed? Is there any preventive maintenance that XYZ will have to perform?

- Describe your company's policy and capabilities regarding system upgrades, new releases, and enhancements. Please state what is covered under your maintenance and support agreements and what portions are not.
- Describe in detail your available support options.
- Does your company support a User's Group? Describe the relationship of your company with the User Group. How often per year do they meet?
- How often does your company publish a newsletter?
- Provide a complete description of how your company will provide implementation and support services to international locations.

6.4 Experience

Briefly (in one page or less) describe your largest or most significant installation to date and the experience it provided you that you can leverage with XYZ. Your answer should indicate the initial size of the installation, the amount of integration, and your specific role in the installation (including resources allocated).

6.5 Implementation Plan

Prospective vendors must provide the following information:

- Describe your system implementation planning process.
- Describe your installation/implementation procedures.
- What is a typical implementation time frame? Please show individual events and time frames for each.
- What are the risks associated in this time frame, and how can the time frames be adjusted to meet the required objectives?
- What role would you play in the implementation?
- How much of the system could be installed by November 1?

6.6 Thought Leadership

Because workforce management technologies are fundamental to the success of a rapidly growing customer support operation, explain how you could provide leadership to XYZ by providing advanced workforce management functionality. How do you remain "ahead of the curve" in staying abreast of innovative features and functions?

6.7 References

Please provide a minimum of three customer references. The following characteristics are desired:

- Large call centers (500+ agents)
- Call centers with multiple sites

(continued)

SAMPLE RFP (*cont.*)

- Functionality (Similar to above requirements)
- Customization
- Integration with other technologies
- Self-sufficient organization

7   Costs

7.1   Initial Costs

Initial Pricing Scope

The initial proposal should outline a price quote and all pricing options available to support the following:

- 200 simultaneous clients
- Multisite (12 sites, each with one ACD)
- Concurrent international user licenses

Complete pricing schedules should be provided that represent the complete cost of ownership for each proposed solution. This schedule must detail specific products and support to be provided as well as the amounts and timing of payments. If appropriate, this should include:

Software

- Cost per client workstation
- Cost per simultaneous user
- Cost per module
- Cost per site
- Cost per server
- Cost for additional tools:
  - Report writers
  - Administrator tools
  - APIs
  - Design tools
  - Data replication tools
  - Other
- Other

Hardware

- Required
- Hardware costs
- Optional hardware costs
- Other

Additional Services

Vendors should provide pricing data for any services not included as part of the software or support purchase. These may include training, implementation support, ongoing consultation, and so on.

Pricing Options

Vendors are encouraged to be creative in their pricing structures. Examples may include, but are not limited to: site licensing, stepped licensing (e.g., per 100 users), complete package pricing, and so on. More than one proposed pricing structure per solution is acceptable.

7.2 Long-Term Costs

Support and Other Long-Term Costs

Please state all costs in dollars not percentages. Assume 24 x 7 support and explain the nature of this support (e.g., pager, third party, etc.). Document basis for support cost increases and maximum increases for the next five years.

- Fixed annual rate
- Usage charges (e.g., per call, per issue, per page, etc.)
- Onsite support rates
- User group fees
- Bulletin board use fees
- System upgrades
- Bug fixes

Please provide all other long-term costs associated with maintaining this technology.

7.3 Payment Options

Prospective vendors are encouraged to include payment option information.

Vendor Site Demo

The vendor site demo involves having members of your project team visit each vendor to receive a demonstration of its product, which provides the project team with the opportunity to evaluate the company and its resources firsthand. This research method can be very beneficial in determining the competency and capability of the vendors.

There are several benefits in using the vendor site demo research method. The following list provides an overview of these benefits:

Seeing the product: It is very difficult to visualize a product without actually seeing it. By examining the product on site, you can verify that the product exists and isn't what is often referred to as "vaporware." In addition, it provides you with a chance to see how usable the user interface is for the product.

Evaluate the vendor: By visiting a vendor's headquarters, you can get a better feel for the vendor's company culture, professionalism, and spending habits. You can also determine what the work atmosphere is like, the caliber of people working for the company, whether employees are happy, and the competency of the managers. Face-to-face meetings are the best way to find out what the staff is like. This is similar to interviewing someone before hiring him. You wouldn't want to hire a person without meeting him first to determine if he will fit in. This method allows you to interview the vendor's people to see if you can work with them. It's better to find this out now than after you have signed contracts.

Importance of your business: When you visit a vendor's headquarters, you will get a feel for how important your business is to the vendor based on who meets with you. If the CEO works you into his schedule, you can be sure he values your business. If any of the chief executives meet with you, you can be sure your business is important to them. If you are not able to meet with anyone except the account representative and a few of the vendor's technical analysts, this is a warning flag that your business is not that important. Although it isn't always critical that you are one of the vendor's most important customers, it is good to know where you stand during the Evaluation phase. You might select vendors with comparable products based on the fact that you are more important to one vendor's business than the other's. This can give you more leverage when asking for improvements to their products.

Evaluate the vendor's support capabilities: If you visit a vendor's headquarters, take the time to meet the support group and have the group members explain how they support their customers. This can give you a good idea of what the support will be like if you select this vendor. A call center staffed by only two people for a company with several hundred customers is a sure sign that you will not receive adequate support. If a company outsources its support, the service you receive probably won't be as good as that you would receive from an internal support group. Another good indicator of a vendor's support capabilities is how the company tracks and escalates calls and issues. If this is done manually on paper as opposed to being computerized, you know that the support group's reporting structure is not capable of informing the company of its critical problems immediately.

Evaluate the vendor's technical knowledge: It is essential that you have a very technical person on your project team to accompany you when visiting a vendor. Let him meet with the technology groups to evaluate their technical competency. It is not necessary for everyone to attend this meeting as technical talk can quickly become foreign to most people. Rely on your technical analysts to let you know whether the vendor is capable of delivering the technology that it says it can.

There are also a number of drawbacks to using the vendor site demo research method. The following list discusses a few of these drawbacks:

High costs: Flying several members of your project team to multiple vendor sites can get expensive. Some project managers reduce the vendor list to three or four before visiting their sites. This can save money and still allow you to enjoy the benefits of seeing these operations in person.

Less control: You have less control over dialogue between the vendor and your project team in face-to-face meetings. Written communication can be managed, but controlling everything that is said is sometimes difficult. Just to illustrate how much damage can be done by a slip of the tongue, I once had a project team member tell a vendor that the technology acquisition process was just a formality and that the vendor pretty much had the deal already. You can imagine what that single statement did to our negotiating leverage. Information is key in negotiations. For this reason, you need to do whatever you can as a project manager to control what is said to the vendors.

Scheduling challenges: Flying around the country visiting multiple vendors can take time. Add scheduling challenges, and you can significantly delay the project. If you plan to visit each vendor on your list, try to schedule the visits as soon as possible.

TIPS

✔ Have all project team members that are involved in the strategic partnership evaluation attend the vendor site visit. It is important that you have the project team members attend all or none of the vendor site visits; otherwise, you are not fairly evaluating vendors.

✔ To get the most out of vendor site visits, schedule them well in advance. Agree on an agenda early so the vendor's account representative will have time to coordinate schedules to allow you to accomplish all of your objectives.

✔ Send an agenda with your objectives (things that you would like to see or discuss during the site visit). This will ensure that you aren't wasting your time and money by visiting the vendor's site.

✔ In some cases, a last minute site visit can provide you with some interesting information about a vendor. Earlier in my career, I was a project team member for several technology acquisitions. For one project in particular, we were trying to decide which of the remaining two vendors to choose for our technology acquisition. We were interested in seeing how quickly both vendors could react to demands and how important our business was to them. Our project manager called the vendors on a Friday and told them that two of the project team members would be at their offices on Monday morning. He didn't specify why we were coming or what our objectives were. He just told them that we were coming and to be ready. When we arrived at vendor A's office on Monday morning, the staff was ready for us. The vendor's account representative escorted us to a conference room, handed us a packed agenda, and asked if we would like to include anything else on the agenda. We didn't need to add anything, so we proceeded with the agenda that had been put together. The schedule included presentations from key managers about the organization and the vision for the future of the company and the technology. It also included a tour of the office, lunch with key executives, evening activities, and a full set of materials on the organization and its product. The icing on the cake was when the CEO met with us to review a survey of the company's customer satisfaction, which had been conducted by an outside resource.

On Tuesday morning, we proceeded to vendor B's office. When we arrived, it took half an hour for the account representative to retrieve us from the lobby. He escorted us to a conference room and told us he would be back soon. He returned with a programmer who spent the better part of the day trying to set up a demo. We basically spent a whole day sitting in the conference room watching these two people try to get organized. When the day was over, they walked us to the door and said good-bye. What a contrast between meetings. The message was loud and clear. Vendor A valued our business and had its act together. Vendor B on the other hand didn't take us seriously enough to plan ahead even though it had more time to prepare. Needless to say, Vendor A received our business and ended up being a very key strategic partner in our company's success. Although this technique is not always the best approach, it is definitely effective when evaluating a vendor's ability to move quickly, and it's a good way to gauge how important your business is to the vendor.

Vendor On-site Demo

One of the most common methods of researching vendors and their technologies is to have them come to your office and conduct a demonstration of their products. This is the simplest method because it puts all the burden on the vendor.

There are several benefits in using the vendor on-site demo research method. The following list provides an overview of these benefits:

Seeing the product: It is very difficult to visualize a product without actually seeing it. By viewing a product demonstration, you can verify that the product exists and isn't what is often referred to as "vaporware." In addition, it provides you with a chance to see how usable the user interface is for the product.

Greater involvement: If the vendors visit your office for demonstrations, you can invite more people to attend. This provides an opportunity for some of the people to attend that normally wouldn't if the demonstrations were at the vendors' offices. The project sponsor and executive sponsors might be able to work the demonstrations into their schedules if they don't require a significant amount of time. This could benefit the process at a later date because the sponsors will have seen the vendors and the products firsthand, and they will have a better understanding of what they are buying.

Vendor education: Vendors can get a better sense of your organization and requirements if they have the opportunity to visit your company in person. If you are looking for a vendor to customize a solution, a visit to your company will enable the vendor to better understand what you are looking for in a product. The vendor might also be able to suggest other solutions to your business needs if it feels that you are taking the wrong approach. Tour your company's facilities with every prospective vendor, and give them a chance to meet the people who will be using the selected vendor's solution. Give them a chance to spend some time watching the end users do their jobs. The questions the vendor asks of these people could help the vendor adapt its solution to better meet your requirements.

Low cost: Having the vendors visit your site to demonstrate their solutions puts all the costs on the vendor and requires little or no cost on your part.

Timeline: Researching vendors can be very time-consuming. For example, using the RFP research method can take weeks to develop and a month for vendors to respond with a proposal. Add a few weeks to evaluate vendor proposals, and you're up to two months. Vendor conferences, benchmarks/pilots, and vendor customer site visits can also be very time intensive. If you are in a big hurry to select a vendor, you can schedule all the vendors to demonstrate their solutions within a few day's time.

Importance of your business: It's uncommon for the vendor's senior management to attend the first vendor demonstration. If the management does participate in the sales process, it is usually later in the process when the decision is closer to being made. If a senior manager does attend the first vendor demonstration, you can be sure that he sees your business as critical to the success of his company. Although it isn't always critical that you are one of the vendor's most important customers, it is good to know where you stand during the Evaluation phase. You might select vendors with comparable products based on the fact that you are more important to one vendor's business than the other's. This can give you more leverage when asking for improvements to their products.

There are also a number of drawbacks to using the vendor on-site demo research method. The following list discusses a few of these drawbacks:

Scheduling challenges: Scheduling vendors can be challenging and can significantly delay the project. If you plan to have the vendors come on-site to demonstrate their solutions, try to schedule the visits as soon as possible.

Less control: You have less control over dialogue between the vendor and your project team in face-to-face meetings. Written communication can be managed, but controlling everything that is said is sometimes difficult. Just to illustrate how much damage can be done by a slip of the tongue, I once had a project team member tell a vendor that the technology acquisition process was just a formality and that the vendor pretty much had the deal already. You can imagine what that single statement did to our negotiating leverage. Information is key in negotiations. For this reason, you need to do whatever you can as a project manager to control what is said to the vendors.

Vendor costs: Vendors will need to spend more money in the sales effort if they are required to travel to your office. Although this isn't necessarily your problem, you should still be aware of how much money you are expecting vendors to spend during the process.

TIPS

✔ Have all project team members that are involved in the strategic partnership evaluation attend the vendor demonstrations. It is important that you have the project team members attend all or none of the vendor demonstrations; otherwise, you are not fairly evaluating vendors.

✔ To get the most out of vendor on-site visits, schedule them well in advance. Agree on an agenda early so the vendors' account representatives will have time to coordinate demonstrators' schedules to allow them to accomplish all of their objectives for the presentation.

✔ Send an agenda with your objectives (things that you would like to see or discuss during the demonstration). This will ensure that you aren't wasting anyone's time and money. It is also a good idea to break down the agenda into specific topics to be addressed. This will ensure that the vendor makes the best use of everyone's time.

✔ Be prepared to take control of the meeting. I have attended a number of vendor presentations, especially when there is more than one vendor involved in the solution, where the vendors did not adhere to the agenda. They have a tendency to rush into Q&A sessions about where they stand compared to the other vendors in the technology acquisition process and what the terms of the deal should be instead of presenting their products.

Vendor Reference Calls

Making vendor reference calls allows you to ascertain what the vendor's customers have to say about the vendor and its technology.

There are several benefits in using the vendor reference call research method. The following list provides an overview of these benefits:

Low cost: Calling vendor references is one of the most economical research methods that you can use. You can quickly and economically find out whether the vendor lives up to its claims, how the product performs, and what the challenges are in implementing the vendor's technology.

Timeline: Researching vendors can be very time-consuming. For example, using the RFP research method can take weeks to develop and a month for vendors to respond with a proposal. Add a few weeks to evaluate vendor proposals, and you're up to two months. Vendor conferences, benchmarks/pilots, and vendor customer site visits can also be very time intensive. If you are in a big hurry to select a vendor, you can call the vendor's references to research both the company and its product very quickly.

Vendor customer satisfaction: If you want to know what the vendor is like to work with and whether its customers are happy with its customer service, calling the vendor's customers is an efficient way to get this important feedback in a short period of time.

Vendor integrity: Calling the vendor's customers enables you to find out whether the vendor lives up to its promises. Salespeople can make their company and product sound pretty attractive. Calling references allows you to validate their claims and ensure that you are getting what you expect if you choose that particular vendor.

Experience: Certain information is only apparent once you have experience working with a vendor and its technology. Find out what others have to say about the vendor. Learn from their experiences. This can save you from making a bad decision based on false information or hollow promises.

Decisions: Find out how other companies made their decisions. Why did they choose a particular vendor, and what was the deciding factor? Was it a close call or was one of the vendors the clear leader? What research methods did they use during their technology acquisition process? Did they use a competing product prior to using the current one? Knowing how other companies chose their vendors can help you understand what was important to them. Keep in mind that their business needs might be very different from yours.

Differences: The vendor's reference companies might have uncovered major differences that you haven't yet uncovered. This is even more likely if the reference companies are experienced with the technology and you are not. You might want to ask the reference companies what the key difference was between the vendors they chose from. The answer to this question could open your eyes to something significant that you had previously missed.

Contacts: You might establish mutually beneficial relationships with the contacts you make during the reference calls. These can be valuable if the company is similar to your company.

There is also a drawback to using the vendor reference call research method—objectivity. The references that you receive will not be random selections. Vendors will only give you references from happy customers. However, wouldn't you do the same? Keep this in mind when calling these references. Make sure you find out about both the positives and negatives of working with this vendor and its technology.

TIPS

✔ Be very specific about the types of references you would like from the vendor. You can specify this in the RFP if you are using that research method. The more similar the references are to your organization, the better the information will be that you receive from them. If you are a very large organization, you wouldn't want a small startup company as a reference. On the flip side, if you are a very small startup company, you wouldn't want a very large company as a reference. Both types of organizations have very different business models, needs, and challenges.

✔ Have all project team members that are involved in the strategic partner-ship evaluation attend the vendor reference calls. It is important that you have the project team members attend all or none of the vendor reference calls; otherwise, you are not fairly evaluating vendors. If you must divide the work, assign one reference for each vendor to a project team member. This will still allow them to be fair and evaluate all vendors equally.

✔ I recommend that you call at least three references for each vendor to see if there are any common issues.

Vendor Customer Site Visit

One of the best methods for researching a vendor and its technology is to visit one of the vendor's existing customer sites. This will enable you to examine the solution firsthand and find out what the people using it think about it.

There are several benefits in using the vendor customer site visit research method. The following list provides an overview of these benefits:

Seeing the product: It is very difficult to visualize a product without actu-ally seeing it. By examining the product at a customer site, you can verify that the product exists and isn't what is often referred to as "vaporware." In addition, it provides you with a chance to see how usable the user interface is for the product.

New ideas: You might get some good ideas from the vendor's customer (even ones that don't pertain to this acquisition). These can be especially beneficial if the company is similar to your company. There are usually several ways to address a business need. Visiting other companies with the same business need can provide you with new ideas about how to best address your business need.

Vendor customer satisfaction: If you want to know how the vendor is to work with and whether customers are happy with its customer service, visiting the vendor's customers is one way to get this important feedback on the vendor's customer service.

Vendor integrity: Visiting the vendor's customers enables you to find out whether the vendor lives up to its promises. Salespeople can make their company and product sound pretty attractive. Talking directly to the vendor's customers allows you to validate its claims and ensure that you are getting what you expect if you choose that particular vendor.

Experience: Certain information is only apparent once you have experience working with the vendor and their technology. Find out what others have to say about the vendor. Learn from their experiences. This can save you from making a bad decision based on false information or hollow promises.

Decisions: Find out how other companies made their decisions. Why did they choose a particular vendor, and what was the deciding factor? Was it a close call or was one of the vendors the clear leader? What research methods did they use during their technology acquisition process? Did they use a competing product prior to using the current one? Knowing how other companies chose their vendors can help you understand what was important to them. Keep in mind that their business needs might be very different from yours.

Differences: The vendor's reference companies might have uncovered major differences that you haven't yet uncovered. This is even more likely if the reference companies are experienced with the technology and you are not. You might want to ask them what the key difference was between the vendors they had to choose from. Their answer to this question could open your eyes to something significant that you had previously missed.

Contacts: You might establish mutually beneficial relationships with the contacts you make during the reference calls. These can be valuable if the company is similar to your company.

There are also a number of drawbacks to using the vendor customer site visit research method. The following list discusses a few of these drawbacks:

Time: It can take weeks to plan and conduct site visits to vendor customer sites. You should visit the same number of customer sites for each vendor in order to remain fair in your evaluation.

Costs: It can be very costly to send several project team members to multiple vendor customer sites. However, if the technology solution is a large purchase, it may be wise to use this research method. If the purchase is small, you might not be able to justify the costs of this research method.

Objectivity: The vendor's customer sites that you visit will not be random selections. Vendors will only send you to happy customers. However, wouldn't you do the same? Keep this in mind when visiting these customer sites. Make sure you find out about both the positives and negatives of working with this vendor and its technology.

TIPS

✔ Have all project team members that are involved in the strategic partnership evaluation attend the vendor customer site visits. It is important that you have the project team members attend all or none of the visits; otherwise, you are not fairly evaluating vendors. If they can't attend all vendor customer site visits, they shouldn't visit any of them.

✔ It isn't a bad idea to have the vendor account representative attend the site visit to act as a chaperone for the group. If the vendor really wants your business, it will make sure its account representative attends.

✔ Be very specific about the types of vendor customers that you would like to visit. The more similar the vendor's customers are to your organization, the better the information will be that you receive from them. If you are a very large organization, you wouldn't want to visit a small startup company. On the flip side, if you are a very small startup company, you wouldn't want to visit a very large company. Both types of organizations have very different business models, needs, and challenges.

✔ It is a good public relations gesture to bring some small gifts to the vendor's customer site. For example, bring coffee mugs or shirts bearing your corporate logo.

✔ If the vendor account representative is in attendance, try to arrange some time with the customer without the vendor account representative present in order to get candid feedback about the vendor and the product. After having used this approach in the past, I was very surprised at the difference in the customer once the vendor wasn't present. When the vendor account representative had left the room, the customer freely discussed all the problems the company was having with the performance of the vendor's technology and how unresponsive the vendor had been in resolving the issue. If we hadn't requested time alone with the vendor's customer, we might not have received this candid feedback on the vendor's service.

✔ If the vendor's customer shows an interest, you might invite the customer to your company for a visit. You might be able to generate a mutually beneficial relationship with the company where you share ideas and information. This opportunity can even grow into co-marketing relationships if the situation is right.

✔ It is inevitable that you will eventually be invited to an informal get-together with the vendor account representative. This meeting can be in the form of a lunch, dinner, a sporting event, golf, or any other activity that will allow the vendor account representative to build a relationship with you and your project team. As stated earlier, this is common when traveling with the vendor's account representative. I recommend that you do not order alcohol unless the vendor suggests it. Also, people tend to act unprofessional when they consume too much alcohol. If your project team members do consume alcohol, make sure they keep it to a minimum. An even better option is to stipulate that none of the team members consume alcohol when on business. This will eliminate the possibility of it causing unnecessary problems.

Vendor Conference

A vendor conference is an excellent way to research vendors while creating a competitive environment between vendors. A vendor conference is a series of back-to-back meetings where all vendors are in attendance and take turns presenting their solutions.

There are several benefits in using the vendor conference research method. The following list provides an overview of these benefits:

Timeline: Although vendor conferences are not the quickest research method, they are also not very time intensive. Planning can be delegated to administrative personnel, allowing you and your team to focus on the other research methods. Once the planning and scheduling is complete, the conference itself is a very efficient way to see multiple vendor presentations in a short period of time.

Competition: A vendor conference is a great way to create a more competitive environment between vendors. Vendors rarely see their competitors except at industry conferences where there are few serious buyers present. This is an opportunity for them to see their competition and meet them face-to-face while competing for your business.

Comparison: A vendor conference provides an efficient way to compare vendors. Because there is little time between presentations, other vendors remain fresh in your mind, and you can easily evaluate which vendor and solution is superior. If anything, it can be a good way to separate the best from the mediocre. You might be able to eliminate some of the vendors from the process after the vendor conference and use the other research methods to evaluate the remaining vendors more closely.

Costs: A vendor conference can be a very cost-effective method of researching vendors. Most of the costs fall on the vendors.

Greater involvement: If the vendor conference is held near your office, you can invite more people to attend. This presents an opportunity for some of the people to attend that normally wouldn't. The project sponsor and executive sponsors should attend the vendor conference. This can be beneficial later on in the process because the sponsors will have met the vendor and have had a chance to evaluate the vendor in person.

Seeing the product: It is very difficult to visualize a product without actually seeing it. By examining the product during a vendor presentation, you verify that the product exists and isn't what is often referred to as "vaporware." In addition, a vendor conference provides you with a chance to see how usable the user interface is for the product.

Vendor education: If you host the vendor conference near your offices, vendors can get a better sense of your organization and its requirements if they have the opportunity to visit your company in person. If you are looking for a vendor to customize a solution, this will enable the vendor to better understand what you are looking for in the product. The vendor might also be able to suggest other solutions for your business need if it feels that you are taking the wrong approach. Tour your company's facilities with each vendor and give each of them a chance to meet the people who will be using the selected vendor's solution. Have the vendors spend some time watching end users do their jobs. The questions the vendors ask of these people could help them adapt their solution to better meet your requirements.

Importance of your business: It's not required that a vendor's senior management attend the vendor conference. If a senior manager does attend the vendor conference, you can be sure that the vendor sees your business as critical to the success of its company. Although it isn't always critical that you are one of the vendor's most important customers, it is good to know where you stand during the Evaluation phase. You might select vendors with comparable products based on the fact that you are more important to one vendor's business than the other's. This can give you more leverage when asking for improvements to the product.

There are also a number of drawbacks to using the vendor conference research method. The following list discusses a few of these drawbacks:

Scheduling challenges: It can be challenging to schedule vendor conferences so that timetables will work for all vendors and attendees. If you schedule vendor conferences well in advance, you will have a better chance of producing a successful vendor conference. Vendors will be able to send the right people and prepare a better presentation if you give them adequate notice.

Less control: You have less control over dialogue between the vendor and your project team in face-to-face meetings. Written communication can be managed, but controlling everything that is said is sometimes difficult. Just to illustrate how much damage can be done by a slip of the tongue, I once had a project team member tell a vendor that the technology acquisition process was just a formality and that the vendor pretty much had the deal already. You can imagine what that single statement did to our negotiating leverage. Information is key in negotiations. For this reason, you need to do whatever you can as a project manager to control what is said to the vendors.

Vendor costs: Vendors will need to spend more money in their sales effort if they are required to travel to your office. Although this isn't necessarily your problem, you should still be aware of how much money you are expecting the vendors to spend during the process.

TIPS

✔ Hold the vendor conference off-site at a hotel with conference room facilities. This offloads coordination and equipment setup and allows the vendor to stay in the hotel where the conference is being held. It is also convenient for informal meetings to take place at the hotel restaurant.

✔ At a minimum, have all project team members that are involved in the strategic partnership evaluation attend the vendor conference. It is important that you have the project team members attend all or none of the vendor presentations; otherwise, you are not fairly evaluating vendors.

✔ To get the most out of vendor conferences, schedule them well in advance. Communicate the agenda and objectives early so the vendors have adequate time to prepare a quality presentation.

✔ Send an agenda with your objectives (things that you would like to see or discuss during the presentation). This will ensure that you aren't wasting anyone's time and money.

✔ With your project team and nonproject team attendees, discuss what to say and what not to say during the vendor conference. Even though you covered this in your project kick-off meeting, it isn't a bad idea to review the agreed-upon terms with everyone again prior to the vendor conference. These can also be documented and sent to your attendees with the agenda prior to the vendor conference.

Benchmark/Pilot

A benchmark or pilot is a test of the solution in order to answer specific questions. For example, if the system has never been scaled to the amount of data, transactions, or users that your implementation requires, you might conduct a benchmark to test the system's performance when scaled to your expected volumes. Any questions that are left unanswered can be considered risks of failure in your project. These unanswered questions are called assumptions. If you have identified any assumptions that could severely impact the Return on Investment (ROI), you can minimize the risks by testing these assumptions with a benchmark or pilot.

There are several benefits in using the benchmark/pilot research method. The following list provides an overview of these benefits:

Proof of concept: A benchmark or pilot can help you determine whether the vendor's technology will functionally do what the vendor says it will do. This is especially important if the technology is new and unproven.

Proof of performance and scalability: A benchmark or pilot can help you determine if the system can operate within an acceptable performance level and whether you will be able to scale the system to grow with your business.

Proof of technology: A benchmark or pilot can help you verify that the technology is sound. Testing a solution can help you determine how experienced the vendor is with the technology. It can also help you discover whether the vendor's product is using a new technology that has not been previously implemented.

Seeing the product: It is very difficult to visualize a product without actually seeing it. By testing a solution, you can verify that the product exists and isn't what is often referred to as "vaporware." In addition, it provides you with a chance to see how usable the user interface is for the product.

Test your environment: If your computing environment is unique, one benefit of conducting a benchmark or pilot is that you can simulate your environment to see how the vendor's product reacts.

Experience: In conducting a benchmark or pilot, you will gain experience installing, setting up, using, and evaluating the vendor's product. This can be a good education for your staff.

There are also a number of drawbacks to using the benchmark/pilot research method. The following list discusses a few of these drawbacks:

Time: It can take weeks to plan and conduct a benchmark or pilot of a vendor's product. If you are benchmarking or piloting multiple vendors' products, it will take even longer. Before using this research method, be aware that it can take up to twice as long as planned to run a benchmark or pilot.

Costs: It can be very costly to send several project team members to attend a benchmark test. If you are hosting the benchmark or pilot at your site, this cost can be reduced. The costs can be very significant if you need to rent or lease facilities or hardware in order to mimic your environment during the benchmark or pilot.

Scheduling challenges: It can be challenging to schedule benchmarks or pilots so that the appropriate vendors and attendees can be present. If you schedule them well in advance, you will have a better chance of producing a successful benchmark or pilot. Vendors will be able to send the right people and prepare a better presentation if you give them adequate notice.

Vendor costs: Vendors will need to spend more money in their sales effort if they are required to travel to your office or a third-party location to conduct benchmarking or piloting. Although this isn't necessarily your problem, you should still be aware of how much money you are expecting vendors to spend during the process.

TIPS

✔ Be very specific when you define your benchmark/pilot objectives and how you will measure what you are trying to prove. If at all possible, include the specific numbers that will constitute an acceptable measurement for each area of the product being evaluated in the benchmark or pilot. This will keep your staff and the vendor focused on the task at hand.

✔ Try to benchmark the product at the vendor's site on its hardware if possible. This will minimize the vendor's costs and the chance of failure due to logistics or setting up a benchmark or pilot at a remote location. If there are issues or questions, the development staff will be in close proximity. The second best option is to use your hardware at your site. This will allow you to include more technology professionals in the benchmark or pilot. This option can be a challenge if there are limited resources to use for the benchmark or pilot.

✔ Try to get benchmark information through the vendor's customers or a third party instead of spending the time and money to do it yourself. Why test something that has already been tested and proven? If you can leverage other companies' efforts, you will save a considerable amount of time and money and achieve the same results.

The following checklist is provided as an aid to help you complete the tasks necessary for the Research process.

RESEARCH PROCESS CHECKLIST

❑ *Adequate research methods have been employed.*

❑ *Vendors and their technologies have been thoroughly and fairly researched.*

❑ *Research results are clearly and consistently documented.*

THE VENDOR SALES TEAM

Vendor sales teams can range from a team of one to a team of several. There are several roles that are common to vendor sales teams including account management, technical specialist, sales management, and executive management.

The account management role is usually the key point of contact between the customer and the vendor. The account manager is the quarterback for the sales team and is ultimately accountable for winning your business. His compensation is usually tied to his sales performance, whereas the other vendor sales team members are often salaried employees. For this reason, the account manager has the highest personal stake in winning your business. The primary objective of the account manager is to win new and repeat business. In order to accomplish this task, he must build relationships with his prospects and customers. He is responsible for becoming educated in his customer's business and then educating the customer on how his company's products and services can help the customer become successful.

There is usually a technical specialist involved in the sales process as well. The title of this individual is not as important as the role that he plays on the sales team. His objective is to communicate how the vendor's technology is built and how it can be integrated into the customer's environment. The technical specialist also provides answers to the customer's technical analysts about the vendor's technology. Although some account managers are quite technical, their primary job is to focus on relationships and manage the sales process. The technical specialist, on the other hand, is responsible for knowing his technology inside-out and being able to communicate technical information to nontechnical and technical customers. One other critical responsibility that the technical specialist has is to establish the credibility of the technical competency of the vendor's staff. Nothing scares a customer away faster than having to deal with a sales team that is not very knowledgeable about current and upcoming technologies. Customers want to know that they are partnering with a vendor that can provide them with enabling technology that doesn't allow their competition an advantage.

Sales management plays a behind-the-scenes role in the sales process. The sales managers are responsible for developing sales strategies and hiring, firing, and managing the sales force. Often, they will get involved in the sales process for key prospects. In almost all cases, they become more involved during the Negotiation process. During negotiations, they usually have the authority to make the final decisions about the terms of the agreement. On some occasions, they will escalate an issue to the executive management, but they try to keep this additional step to a minimum, as it is their responsibility to work these issues out.

Although it is less common, executive management can also play a role on the vendor's sales team. When your company is labeled as a strategic customer, the members of the executive management team will be very aware of the project's status throughout the process and often will get involved to show the customers how important their business is to them. By strategic customer, I mean that the vendor sees winning your business as vital to its ability to remain competitive in the market.

This is the best situation to be in as a customer because the vendor will typically give you a better than normal deal. Keep your eyes open to see how much involvement there is from the vendor's executive management team in order to understand how important it is to the company to win your business.

Vendor Character and Integrity

One very important reason to establish a face-to-face relationship with the vendor sales team is to evaluate the character and integrity of its members.

A vendor's character is usually consistent throughout its company. If you find that the vendor sales team is very aggressive, you will often find that the company in general is aggressive. If you find the vendor sales team to be very customer satisfaction driven, you will most likely find that the vendor in general has high customer satisfaction ratings. Use the technology acquisition process to get a good read on the character of the vendor sales team in terms of aggressiveness, customer satisfaction, technical competency, sense of urgency, commitment, open-mindedness, and vision.

Another important detail that you can learn from the technology acquisition process is how much integrity the vendors have. Do they deliver on their promises? You will be giving vendors many deadlines throughout the process. This is a chance to see how reliable they are. Additionally, do they make promises that they can't keep? Do they shoot from the hip (answer questions when they don't really know the answer)? Or do they say they don't know and that they will find out as soon as possible? If they do say they will follow up with an answer, do they, or do you have to remind them? It is often easier to determine if there is a lack of integrity. Warning signals can come from many different areas, such as ignoring your rules on how to participate in the acquisition process. Another warning signal might be an account manager who constantly criticizes other vendors instead of focusing on what his company can bring to the table. In extreme cases, bribery or blackmail are definite signs of a lack of integrity. It is important that you select a vendor who will operate with integrity.

Use the technology acquisition process to gain a good understanding of the character and integrity of the vendor. This will help to ensure that you partner with a vendor who shares your values and will be easy to work with over the years.

Relationships

It is important to establish relationships with members of the vendor's sales team. They will be responsible for your account once the sales process is over. If you take the time to cultivate a good working relationship with the account manager, he can often champion your cause within his organization. Additionally, account managers are great sources of information and contacts. They meet with new people on a daily basis and find out what is going on in the industries in which they specialize. If you have questions about specific companies or industries, an account manager may be able to introduce you to people who are in those companies and industries, or who are very knowledgeable about them.

When building relationships with vendor sales teams, it is important to communicate with them on a regular basis during and after the technology acquisition. Keep them updated on the timelines and your team's progress. It is also important to make sure that you are treating the vendors fairly. They will respect your decisions if they know that they were given a fair chance to compete.

4

Evaluation

Initiation → Planning → Research → Evaluation → Negotiation → Implementation → Operation

At this stage of the technology acquisition process, you have thoroughly researched the vendors and their technologies. Now it's time to evaluate vendors objectively and make a decision.

This chapter outlines a process that can be used to aid in the decision-making process. By following this process, you will be able to make a more educated decision about which vendor and technology is best for your company's needs.

THE EVALUATION PROCESS

The Evaluation process consists of four potential subprocesses: structured research methods, unstructured research methods, decision-making, and communicating results to vendors (Figure 4-1).

Structured research evaluation methods include methods that help objectify the decision-making process by breaking down the overall decision into many small decisions. This systematic approach produces a vendor score, which represents how well each vendor matches your company's requirements.

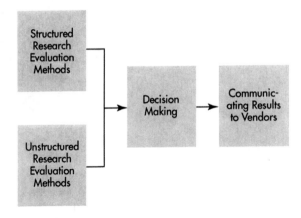

Figure 4-1: Evaluation subprocesses

Unstructured research evaluation methods are not systematic and do not produce a solution for which vendor is best for your company. However, this method does produce information that will aid in the subjective side of the decision-making process.

Decision making involves using a particular process to arrive at a decision. This process includes gaining consensus, forming a project team recommendation, and presenting the recommendation.

Communicating the results to the vendor is not always the most enjoyable part of the process. This chapter discusses how to inform the vendors of your company's decision and what to look out for when doing so.

The primary goal of the Research phase is to gather the information required to make a decision about which vendor and technology will best meet your business needs. Once you have completed this phase, you can then begin the decision-making process. There are two types of decisions: objective and subjective. Each research method provides an objective or subjective decision-making environment (Table 4-1).

Structured Research Evaluation Methods

An objective decision is one that is made without human judgement. In other words, there is no element of the decision that is left to a human decision. Objective decisions are those that use a set of criteria that produce a decision. For example, if one of your criterion was for the vendor to have over $1 billion in revenue, the prospective vendors would either meet that requirement or not. Structured research

Table 4-1: Research Methods for Decision Making

Provide Objective Decision Making	Provide Subjective Decision Making
External Research	Vendor Site Demo
External Assessment	Vendor On-site Demo
Request for Proposal (RFP)	Vendor Reference Calls
Benchmark/Pilot	Vendor Customer Site Visit
	Vendor Conference

evaluation methods are designed to produce an objective decision. The following list contains information on the objective research methods:

- *External research:* When you purchase research externally, you should look for a researcher who provides detailed information that compares vendors as objectively as possible. You shouldn't leave it up to the researcher to just state which vendor is superior. Researchers must justify their recommendation with detailed research.

- *External assessment:* If the right model is used to assess the competency of the vendors, this research method can provide a very specific differentiation between vendors and how they operate their businesses.

- *Request for Proposal (RFP):* The RFP is the primary research method used to create an objective comparison between vendors. All vendors are required to respond in the same format, creating a clear distinction between each vendor. This allows the vendor scoring matrix to be used in scoring vendors and their abilities to meet the requirements stated in the RFP.

- *Benchmark/Pilot:* You should not conduct a benchmark/pilot unless you have very specific questions to answer. For example, if you are testing performance, specific measurements of performance can be taken during the benchmark/pilot.

Unstructured Research Evaluation Methods

A subjective decision is made using human judgement. An example of a subjective decision is determining which vendor has the best customer service. Because customer service is very hard to quantify, answering this question requires a judgement call. Unstructured research methods provide an environment for subjective decision making. The following list contains information about subjective research methods:

- *Vendor site demo:* A vendor site demo allows you to ask specific questions, but, for the most part, only produces a subjective decision. It is inevitable that each vendor will be asked different questions in a different context.

- *Vendor on-site demo:* On-site demos can be very beneficial in gaining an understanding of the vendor's product and personnel. On the other hand, it doesn't produce a very objective differentiation between vendors. It is difficult to ensure that each vendor is being evaluated fairly and objectively with this type of research method. Salesmanship can make a vendor look better than it really is.

- *Vendor reference calls:* Reference calls generate comments based on the opinion of the vendor's customer. It is difficult to determine the quality of the individual or the biases involved in a person's feedback when talking to a stranger over the phone.

- *Vendor customer site visits:* Similar to the vendor reference call, most of the comments you will receive will be based on subjective opinions of the vendor's customers. Additionally, in most cases, they will not be using the technology in exactly the same manner. Because there are so many variables involved, it is difficult to get an objective decision based on this research method.

- *Vendor conference:* The vendor conference provides each vendor with a fair chance to demonstrate its ability to meet your business requirements. Although this method is fair, any decisions made using this research method will still be based on the subjective opinions of the attendees.

Now that each research method and whether it produces an objective or subjective decision has been introduced, let's discuss another tool that can be used to produce a subjective decision. This tool is called a scenario. Using the scenario method, you create a diagram illustrating the decision with each prospective vendor as a possible answer. You then add to each vendor the potential outcomes of selecting it as the vendor of choice. Figure 4-2 illustrates how this diagram might look.

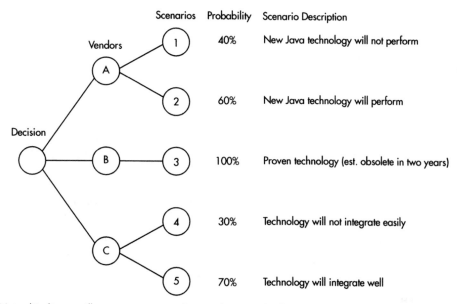

Note: this diagram illustrates a scenario diagram from a technology perspective. You can create these diagrams from other perspectives (for example: business stability, timeline risk, or business case success potential).

Figure 4-2: Scenario planning

Creating a scenario diagram can help to visualize the decision at hand. Once you have created your diagram and have determined the probability of each outcome if a particular vendor was chosen, you can start to plan out each scenario and determine which is best for your company. Taking the time to clearly document the impacts (positive and negative), costs versus benefits, return on investment, long-term results, and assumptions for each scenario on your current business can be very helpful to a decision maker. This tool is primarily subjective but can be objective if, for example, you were to use a formula that multiplies the two-year return on investment by the probability or some other quantitative measurement to provide one scenario with a better score than the rest.

Decision Making

All of the project team's effort up to this point, defining the requirements and researching the vendors and their technologies, is focused on leading the team to a decision of which vendor to select. Ultimately, this will be a subjective decision. It is the project team's job to objectify the decision as much as possible and provide quality subjective comparisons that will help the final decision maker make as educated a decision as possible given the circumstances. Any surprises that surface after the decision is made will reflect poorly on the project team. The following case study provides an example of how surprises can affect the project.

Case Study

SURPRISES THAT SURFACE AFTER THE DECISION

On a previous technology acquisition, Jack's team had made a strong recommendation, and the project sponsor ended up supporting that decision. The financials of each option played heavily in the decision. A week after the project sponsor had received approval from executive management, a project team member came to Jack with a $50,000 charge for a piece of hardware that was needed to connect the vendor's solution to the company's network. This project team member hadn't mentioned this cost or requirement to Jack previously and should have because it was in that project team member's area of expertise. You can imagine how Jack felt and how he was perceived when he had to go back to the project sponsor and tell him that he needed another $50,000.

The lesson learned from this situation is to make sure that every stone is overturned and that all aspects of the deal are visible to the decision makers. They are relying, sometimes completely, on the information that the project team provides to make their final decision. Don't let them down by missing critical components of the deal that will eventually surface and create problems.

LESSON LEARNED
Make sure you understand every detail regarding the vendor and the solution.

Typically, you want the project team to achieve consensus and select a vendor prior to presenting the results to the project sponsor. I recommend setting up an all-day off-site meeting with the project team members to review the results of the research and discuss each team member's analysis of the results. An example of an agenda for this meeting might be:

• Review the agenda and ground rules

• Outline the research process that was undertaken

- Review the results of each research method

- Review the scenarios

- Review the decision scoring matrix

- Have each project team member present his or her ranking and comments on each vendor

- Build consensus

Be sure that each project team member has read through all of the research and has scored the vendors on the vendor scoring matrix prior to this meeting. Members should bring all of the information gathered during the process to this meeting so that they will have everything needed to make a decision. By the end of the meeting, you need to make sure that everyone agrees on which vendor best meets your business needs. You also need to define which vendors are the team's first, second, and third choices. This can be helpful if something happens to eliminate the first choice vendor later in the process. After the meeting is complete, it is helpful to document the decision-making process in a document called the Vendor Selection Summary. This document can be particularly helpful if someone questions how you selected the vendor of choice later in the process or well after the project has been completed.

TIPS

✔ It can be helpful to have someone who has not been involved in the technology acquisition in any way facilitate the project team meeting to decide on a vendor. This person should have excellent facilitation skills and be competent in managing conflict effectively. One advantage of this approach is that the facilitator will ask questions that the project team may have made assumptions on. This is essential at this point in the process. Anything missed can cause a poor decision by the team. It is better to get everything out on the table and make sure everyone knows everything about each vendor before making the decision.

Once the project team has reached a consensus and has selected a vendor, it is then time to present the recommendation to the project sponsor. When presenting the recommendation, have the entire project team in the room with your project sponsor. The project manager should facilitate the meeting and be sure to introduce members of the project team, state the department they represent, and the role they are playing on the project team. This will give your team members a little exposure for their efforts on the project team.

Once the introductions are complete, you should state the purpose of the meeting, which is to review the Vendor Selection Overview with the project sponsor as well as the agenda for the meeting. Make sure you state that the project team members will present their results and that all questions should be reserved until the document is completely reviewed.

Have a designated leader from each group (functionality, technology, strategic partnership potential, and cost) present the appropriate part of the Research Evaluation section of the Vendor Selection Summary document.

After the research evaluation presentations are complete, the project manager should present the recommendation and then open up the session for questions. Project sponsors will usually have many questions, which is the reason for waiting until the presentation is complete before accepting questions. Questions will sometimes include inquiries about the process that was used and other times may request more details on a particular vendor or score. You should document all questions that cannot be answered in the meeting as action items, and at the end of the meeting, summarize them to ensure you have captured the questions accurately.

To close the meeting, it is a nice gesture to have the project sponsor say a few nice words to the project team members thanking them for their efforts. You should ask the project sponsor if he would be willing to do so prior to the meeting, so that he is prepared.

Generally, the project sponsor will support the project team's recommendation. If the project sponsor does not, make sure you document his concerns about the recommendation and follow up on those concerns to resolve the issues. In the end, the decision is ultimately the project sponsor's responsibility, so the team should support that decision regardless of what it is. Prepare the project team members for this possible turn of events by telling them that you want them to voice their opinions and concerns as rigorously as possible up until the final decision. Once the decision has been made, everyone should respect the project sponsor's decision and support that decision. Remind them that they have done their jobs, and it is now up to the project sponsor to make the final decision.

Communicating Results to Vendors

Communicating the final decision to vendors can be both pleasant and unpleasant. It is fun telling a vendor that it is the vendor of choice; however, it is no fun at all to have to tell the other vendors that they were not chosen. During the process, you begin to build a relationship with the account managers, which sometimes makes it harder to tell them they have lost the deal. Regardless, it is your responsibility to call each account manager individually and give him the news. Don't hide behind a letter or have someone else tell the account managers. This is not the proper way to conduct business. Just give them a call and get it over with. Then follow up with a formal letter. There are a few items that you should consider before calling the vendors.

The nondisclosure agreement (NDA) that you signed earlier in the process is usually a two-way agreement, meaning that you can't share proprietary information about the vendor with a third party, and the vendor can't share proprietary information about your company with a third party. Therefore, be very careful about what you tell a vendor when asked the obvious question about what lost the deal for its company. For example, don't tell other vendors about a new proprietary feature in the chosen vendor's new and unreleased product. This would clearly breach the confidentiality agreement. For this reason, keep your comments very general. For example, you might say "the chosen vendor was a closer match to our requirements" or "the chosen vendor was superior in this general area of functionality." The account manager will naturally push for more information, so understand his position. He is the one that has to go back to his management and explain why the deal was lost.

Some people prefer to keep all vendors in the running until the Negotiation phase is complete and the contract is signed. My preference is to select a vendor first, and negotiate with one vendor at a time. Just make sure that all vendors know that if you cannot reach a deal with the vendor of choice, you will be opening up discussions with other vendors again. Until then, there should be no further contact or selling.

TIPS

✔ Make sure that you clearly inform other vendors that the decision has been made and that you are pursuing another vendor. If negotiations are not successful, you will be opening up communications with other vendors at that time (but no sooner). If this information is not clearly explained, vendors will continue the sales process thinking they can still win the deal. If a vendor comes back with a significantly better offer, don't open up discussions with the company as a result. A better approach is to use that information as leverage with the vendor of choice. If your vendor of choice knows that you have a very attractive deal to fall back on, the company will understand that it has to do everything possible to keep you from bringing the other vendor back to the table.

The following checklist is provided as an aid to help you complete the tasks necessary for the Evaluation process.

EVALUATION PROCESS CHECKLIST

❑ *Research has been evaluated for all vendors.*

❑ *The vendor scoring matrix has been completed.*

❑ *The project team has reviewed all research.*

❑ *The project team has achieved consensus on a vendor.*

❑ *All research evaluation and decision processes have been clearly documented.*

❑ *The project sponsor has approved the decision.*

❑ *The results have been communicated to the vendors verbally and then in written form.*

5

Negotiations

Skillful negotiating is both an art and a science. The science can be taught, but the art can only be obtained through experience or natural instinct. There are many books on the topic of negotiating. The goal of this chapter is not to reinvent the wheel by writing about negotiating skills, but instead to provide you with a framework to manage a negotiation for a successful technology acquisition. Not only will this framework enable you to successfully manage a negotiation, it will also help you understand how to position your company to create a beneficial relationship with the selected vendor.

This chapter also discusses the negotiation team. Roles that need to be played are described as well as the types of people best suited for those roles.

THE NEGOTIATION PROCESS

The Negotiation process consists of three potential subprocesses: negotiation strategy, negotiation planning, and negotiations (Figure 5-1).

Figure 5-1: Negotiation subprocesses

The most important step in successful negotiating is defining your negotiation strategy. Let's begin the Negotiation process by discussing how you should go about determining your strategy.

Planning a negotiation can be difficult due to the unpredictability of the process. There is no telling whether the process will be long and grueling or quick and easy. Provided in this chapter are ways to plan the negotiation to add structure to the process and ensure that all parties have the opportunity to negotiate a beneficial contract for their organization.

After you define your strategy and plan the Negotiation process, it is then time to begin the negotiations. This chapter discusses the events that typically take place during a negotiation.

Negotiation Strategy

You should never begin a Negotiation process without knowing what your negotiation strategy will be. A strategy helps you determine whether the negotiation was successful. Before discussing defining agendas and leverage, let's discuss a trend that is growing in the technology acquisition arena.

Owning versus Using

Many companies have shifted their focus from owning technology to paying to use technology. This shift can be seen in the growth of service revenue, which has increased significantly in the past decade. Vendors are finding more value in establishing a network of users based on long-term subscription fee structures rather than on one or more purchases of product. At the same time, companies need to keep up with the fast pace of change, and owning physical assets can slow them down. Let's look at the two types of vendor-customer relationships in greater detail.

Buyer-Seller Relationship

The traditional relationship between two companies is a buyer-seller relationship. In this arrangement, one company produces a product and the other buys it. Typically this includes a transfer of a physical asset. The buyer then spreads the cost over the expected lifetime of the asset (i.e., depreciation) to minimize the short-term impact of the purchase on the company's annual financial performance. Once the asset is fully depreciated, the buyer then purchases a replacement (not always from the same vendor).

One benefit of the buyer-seller relationship is in the ease of computing the Return on Investment (ROI). This is calculated by measuring the cost of the product and the benefits gained over the life of the product. Another benefit is that the buyer has less dependency on a seller. If the buyer is unhappy with the product, the buyer can buy future products from another company.

One of the drawbacks of the buyer-seller relationship can be seen in the number of products that are replaced prior to being fully depreciated. In other words, the product's life expectancy is greater than reality. Another drawback is that the vendor often spends a lot of time and resources selling the product initially, and then disappears after the sale is complete.

Network-User Relationships

A relationship that is growing in popularity at a tremendous rate is the network-user relationship. In this type of arrangement, one company becomes part of another company's network. These companies are also called Application Service Providers (ASP). Membership to this network can include the transfer of product, services, or even management of a business function. The focus is on long-term relationships where both companies work together to provide a mutually beneficial exchange. An example of this type of relationship is a car lease. Instead of selling an asset to a customer, the product is provided to the customer for a monthly fee for a specific period of time (typically 2-3 years). The buyer pays to use the product instead of owning it. Before the lease expires, the vendor contacts the customer to explore continuing the relationship with a new lease and potentially a new vehicle. The focus shifts from selling a product to providing a function (transportation) to the customer. This causes the vendor to shift its focus toward building a long-term relationship instead of just selling a product every few years.

The benefits of a network-user relationship lie in the partnership that is formed between the two companies. Because the relationship is an ongoing interaction, it forces both companies to work together. Another benefit is that the user is not tied to a product because the product hasn't yet completed its depreciation cycle. The user pays a fee for access to a function instead of owning a product, so it is easier to just switch vendors if needs change or if the user is not happy with the vendor's product. Regardless of who hosts the solution, the user still has the challenge of data conversion when switching to a new system.

One of the drawbacks of the network-user relationship is that the vendor may become too comfortable and not continue to contribute to the relationship on an on-going basis after the initial deal is made.

Agendas

Everyone has an agenda when negotiating. The key in developing a successful strategy is to have a clear understanding of what you want and what the vendor wants. You've probably heard the phrase, "Information is key in successful negotiating." The purpose of defining both companies' agendas is to help you gather the information that you need to build a successful negotiation strategy.

Clearly defining your company's agenda (desired terms of the deal) will help you prepare for the negotiations. You will also be able to put together a plan including negotiation tactics that will enable you to successfully negotiate these terms into the deal.

Be aware that there are always hidden agendas as well. As project manager, it is your job to find out what they are. Be persistent until you have uncovered all expectations and understand what the priorities are.

In a typical negotiation, each company begins by specifying the terms of the deal that each would like. The rest of the negotiation centers around narrowing the gap between the two company's terms until they can both agree on the terms of the deal. By knowing what the vendor wants, you can understand its priorities and use that information to your advantage. For example, if you know that the vendor really wants to be able to use you as a reference as part of the deal, you might use that term as leverage in getting something that you want in return. If you didn't know in advance that the reference was a high priority of the vendor's, you might have conceded that term in the initial offer without negotiating for something in return.

Understanding agendas allows you to negotiate from a position of strength, so that you can ensure that your company gets the best deal possible.

Leverage

Generally, the company with the most leverage in a negotiation gets the better deal. Without leverage, the other company has no reason to concede anything except the standard terms. On the other hand, if you have leverage, you can use it to shape the deal to your liking. Gaining leverage is one of the biggest benefits of going through such a rigorous technology acquisition process. Information provides you with leverage. Gathering this information during the Research phase and creating a competitive environment between vendors is what gives you the most leverage walking into a negotiation. For example, during the Research phase, you might learn that your chosen vendor has recently lost two deals to its top competitor. Contacting the buying companies to find out why they chose another vendor could identify an issue with the product of the vendor you are negotiating with. Bringing this issue up during negotiations will really put the heat on the vendor because the company recently lost two deals for that specific reason. Research the vendor thoroughly, so that you know everything there is to know about the vendor, and you will discover what it can and can't concede during the Negotiation process.

Determine your leverage points. Start by creating a list of leverage points in your favor. An example list might include the following items:

- *Name recognition:* The vendor can use this as a marketing tool.

- *Strategic customer:* The vendor sees your business as critical to the success of its company.

- *Potential future sales:* If you are buying 100 licenses of the vendor's product and there is a good chance that you will purchase 2,000 licenses within the next two years, you can use this future purchase to get volume pricing on the initial 100 licenses.

- *First to a market:* You are the first large customer in a specific market to use this type of technology, and the vendors want to be the first to prove that they can support your type of business.

- *Timing:* If you know that the vendor is in a hurry to close the deal before the books close on the company's fiscal year, you can use that as leverage by delaying until the last minute and forcing the vendor to concede a few important terms before you close the deal.

- *Buyer advantage:* The buyer automatically has leverage based on the fact that the vendor is competing for your business.

By identifying all of the leverage points that you have in dealing with a particular vendor, you will be in a better position to use them in developing your strategy.

What leverage does the vendor have? Knowing what cards the vendor holds allows you to develop counter strategies to minimize the benefits that these leverage points will provide. Create a list of the vendor's leverage points such as the following sample list:

- Your business is not critical to the vendor's success.

- The vendor's product is by far the best solution, and the vendor knows it.

- The vendor's product is by far the lowest priced solution (and the vendor knows it).

- The vendor has limited supply of a product in high demand.

- The vendor knows that you are in desperate need of the technology quickly.

These are just a few examples of the leverage that a vendor might have when dealing with a customer. If you take the time to define these leverage points, you may be able to counter them or eliminate them. For example, in the last sample leverage point, you might decide not to let the vendor know how quickly you need the technology until after the other terms of the deal are agreed upon.

Taking the time to formally document the negotiation strategy can be very beneficial in clarifying what you are trying to accomplish.

Priorities

It is important to know what your priorities are before entering into a negotiation. No two negotiations are exactly the same because different people have different priorities.

If you know that your priority is price, you can concede terms related to quality and time in return for the terms related to price. If your priority is quality, you may negotiate terms that guarantee a certain level of quality and concede terms related to price and time. If your priority is time, you may concede terms related to price and quality in return for terms related to time. It is essential that you know exactly what is important before you enter negotiations.

Another priority may be to develop a strategic partnership with a well run business. In some cases, it may be better for both companies if you pay full price for the technology. This probably sounds crazy, but let me explain. You may be negotiating with a vendor who is small and not financially profitable but who has an edge in technology. The vendor may not have other customers who can help the company remain profitable while providing you with the technology at cost. In this situation, do you really want to partner with a company who is losing money by doing business with you? How do you expect them to fund research and development for future products if they are working for free? Sometimes, it is better to pay a fair price and focus more on the relationship and how the company can improve your business.

It is important to focus on what both companies need in order to be successful. Take these priorities into the negotiation and together figure out how to structure a deal that will satisfy both parties. See the following negotiation strategy template and sample for more information.

Template

NEGOTIATION STRATEGY

SUMMARY
Provides a summary of the process and sets the context for the negotiations.

INITIAL TERMS
Lists key terms of the deal. These are typically pulled from the vendor's proposal. This serves as the starting point for the negotiations.

AGENDAS
Lists the possible agendas for the vendor. For example, you may know that the vendor is losing market share to competitors and is desperately in need of winning your business to maintain credibility.

LEVERAGE
Defines the leverage that exists on both sides of the negotiation.

OBJECTIVES
Lists terms you will try to change during the negotiation. This section describes what you want to accomplish during the negotiation.

STRATEGY
Defines the strategy for negotiating a favorable deal. For example, you may elect to focus on long-term cost reductions instead of short-term costs.

POTENTIAL TACTICS
Defines the tactics that may be used during the negotiation to accomplish the objectives of the negotiation.

NEGOTIATION TEAM AND ROLES
Defines the roles of the team members during the negotiation process.

SAMPLE Negotiation Strategy

1. Summary

The project team has selected AAA Corporation as the vendor of choice. BBB Corporation was a close second, and the project team feels confident that both companies would be able to achieve the objectives of this project. For this reason, the negotiation team has full authority to negotiate the best financial package with either of the two vendors.

2. Initial Terms

The initial terms of the deal from the vendor proposals are listed below:

		AAA Corporation	BBB Corporation
Initial Cost			
	Software	$860K	$ 950K
	Hardware	$ 35K	$ 40K
	Consulting	$ 75K	$ 60K
	Total:	$970K	$1,050K
Ongoing Support Costs			
	Annual Support	$ 30K	$ 25K

3. Agendas

XYZ Agenda:

Negotiate the best financial package.

Vendor Agenda:

- Maximize revenue
- Be the first to gain an international call center customer
- Leverage XYZ's name recognition for future marketing

4. Leverage

XYZ Leverage:

- Name recognition
- Information about competition
- International call centers
- Ability to walk away from the table

Vendor Leverage:

Time

5. Objectives

Negotiate the best financial package with either of the two remaining vendors.

6. Strategy

Leverage the fact that both vendors are capable of meeting our project objectives and that the financial package will be the determining factor in who gets the deal.

7. Potential Tactics

- Give both vendors a last chance to sharpen their pencils and improve their financial package. Then select one vendor and work on improving the package. Inevitably, the vendor who wasn't selected will respond with a significant price reduction as an incentive to bring them back into the game. Use this information as leverage to improve the deal with the selected vendor.
- Create a time-based bidding war

8. Negotiation Team and Roles

- Purchasing Lead: Act as the bad cop and strive for the most aggressive deal
- Project Manager: Act as the good cop and facilitate continued communications
- Business Lead: Communicate the potential future business to the vendor
- Legal: Negotiate with vendor legal staff and advise negotiation team

Negotiation Planning

There is typically a need for two different negotiations. The first is between the decision makers on the key terms of the deal. The second is between the attorneys on the wording of the contracts. When planning a negotiation, you should plan each of these negotiations separately and well in advance.

Decision-Maker Negotiations

The negotiation between the decision makers is the more important of the two negotiations. For this reason, you should plan this negotiation to take place prior to the attorneys' negotiations. If the decision makers are not able to come to an agreement, there will be no need for the attorneys to meet.

When planning the decision-makers' negotiation, it is often helpful to create an environment that enables cooperation. This is why you often hear about deals being made on the golf course. The important factor is not the golf, but that you are socializing with the vendor in a friendly, neutral setting leading up to the discussions of the terms of the new relationship being forged between the two companies.

Try to conduct decision-maker negotiations in face-to-face meetings with the vendor and your negotiation team. Make sure that the vendor's decision maker is also present when this meeting takes place. This allows the vendor's negotiation team to respond to requests in a timely manner.

When planning this type of negotiation, make sure that only the key decision makers are present. This will minimize the distractions and enable the decision makers to focus on the task at hand.

Attorney Negotiations

The attorney negotiations should take place once the key terms of the deal have been agreed on by the decision makers. It is the attorneys' job to ensure that the contracts are worded in a way that is favorable to their company and limits the company's risk as much as possible. Attorneys don't need to meet face-to-face for their negotiations. They will be able to draw up contracts and negotiate changes over the phone and fax.

Because attorneys are very busy and are expensive resources, it is best to plan the negotiations well in advance so that their time can be reserved, and there will be no delays. It is also a good idea to make sure the vendor's legal team will be available to negotiate during the designated time.

Negotiations

What typically happens during the negotiations? Each negotiation is different, but there is a general process that takes place. In this process, both parties state their desired terms. This is followed by a discussion between the parties of the differences or gaps between the two parties' desired terms. Once these gaps are defined, the two parties can begin negotiating to eliminate these gaps. This usually requires that one party concede a term or the term be redefined in a way that both parties can agree on. Often one party will concede a term in return for the other party conceding one of the other terms. Once all of the gaps are removed, an agreement can be reached in which both parties accept the terms of the deal.

There will be times when both parties cannot reach an agreement. When this happens, both parties need to decide whether to continue negotiating or walk away from the deal. If negotiations end, it's time to reinitiate contact with the second vendor of choice and begin the Negotiation process over again. See the following deal sheet template and sample for more information.

Template

DEAL SHEET

Describes the terms of the deal and your objectives in a format that is easy to use during negotiations. The following table can be used as a template for the deal sheet.

#	Term	Initial	Minimum	Goal
1	<Term description>	<term>	<term>	<term>
2	<Term description>	<term>	<term>	<term>
3	<Term description>	<term>	<term>	<term>
4	<Term description>	<term>	<term>	<term>
5	<Term description>	<term>	<term>	<term>

SAMPLE Deal Sheet

The following table represents the vendor's initial bid, XYZ's minimum acceptable terms, and XYZ's goals.

#	Term	Initial	Minimum	Goal
1	Software	860,000	900,000	500,000
2	Hardware	35,000	30,000	30,000
3	Consulting	75,000	70,000	70,000
4	Annual Support Costs	30,000	30,000	30,000
5	Implementation Date	01–Aug	01–Sep	01–Jul

The following checklist is provided as an aid to help you complete the tasks necessary for the Negotiation process.

NEGOTIATION PROCESS CHECKLIST

❑ *A negotiation team has been defined.*

❑ *Roles and responsibilities are clearly defined and communicated to team members.*

❑ *The team has agreed on a negotiation strategy.*

❑ *There is a clear plan for the Negotiation process.*

❑ *The results of the negotiation are clearly documented in contract form.*

❑ *Your company's attorneys have approved the contracts.*

❑ *The project sponsor has approved the contracts.*

THE NEGOTIATION TEAM

The negotiation team is most effective when it is small and has the appropriate people assuming each of the roles. When setting up a negotiation team, you should recognize that there will be input from people outside the negotiation team. The negotiation team should only include the people who will actually be discussing and negotiating the terms of the agreement between the two companies. I recommend that you establish the following roles on your negotiation team: facilitator, legal representative, contract administrator, and decision makers.

Facilitator

The facilitator is usually the project manager. Although this is not always the case, I highly recommend taking this approach. The project manager is the most familiar with the vendor and has already established a relationship with the vendor's account manager during the Research phase. This role requires a person who has good listening skills and thinks before speaking.

During the Negotiation phase, the facilitator should view his role as a peacemaker who is only interested in working out an agreement that will make both companies happy. The facilitator should be the one who keeps the dialogue going with the vendor when tactics call for walking away from the table. A good approach is to tell the account manager for the vendor that the two of you need to work together to bring both decision makers to agreement.

Legal Representative

It is *critical* that every negotiation team include a legal representative. Your company will be entering a legally binding contract with the vendor involving the exchange of product, services, and capital, and therefore should be covered legally. The failure of one party to live up to its end of the bargain can be very damaging to either company.

For this reason, you want a written agreement that clearly states what is expected of each company. You've probably heard the statement "Verbal agreements aren't worth the paper they're written on." Make sure you capture all aspects of the deal in writing and make sure that a legal representative for your company is involved to ensure that correct wording is used. It is also important to have the legal representative negotiate the exit terms with the vendor, which outline how your company can terminate a bad deal if things don't work out with the vendor.

Most companies have a legal staff on-site. These people are not always employees of your company, but instead are usually retained by your company for their services. If you have several legal representatives, request the representative with the most experience in dealing with technology agreements.

You will find that legal resources are always limited and in demand. Make sure you plan ahead and reserve their time well in advance. This will keep your project moving forward and minimize any delays due to scheduling issues.

Contract Administrator

Most companies have designated contract administrators. You should have a contract administrator on your team to manage the legal documentation. Legal representatives are too expensive for this task, so a contract administrator is usually responsible for modifying all agreements and maintaining the history of changes.

If your organization does not have a contract administrator, you need to identify someone to fill this role. If this is the case, look for someone who has good typing skills and a perfectionist mentality.

Decision Makers

The *most* important role on the negotiation team is that of decision makers. When all is said and done, decision makers are the ones who make the final decision to proceed or not to proceed with an agreement. They will ultimately be held accountable for the contents of the agreement. I have seen decision makers terminated because they signed a bad deal costing their company a significant loss in time and resources. You don't want this to happen in your company. They depend on you to make sure that the vendor, technology, and agreement are right for your company.

Decision makers are usually the project sponsors. If the project sponsors on your team are not decision makers, you probably don't have the right project sponsors. They must have the authority to approve the contract. It is very difficult to negotiate if the person with the final approval isn't part of the negotiation team. It requires many more meetings as well as going back and forth between the decision makers and the vendor representatives every time an issue is in question. If you are faced with having a decision maker who is not on the negotiation team, take the time to overcome this obstacle by making sure the decision maker is added to the negotiation team before negotiations begin.

You may find that there are other roles required on your negotiation team depending on the tactics that you employ. At a minimum, you should make sure that the roles previously listed are represented adequately.

6

Implementation

After having thoroughly researched, evaluated, and selected the vendor that was the closest match to your business needs, you then negotiated an agreement that benefits both companies. Now it's time for the vendor to implement its solution within your business.

The Implementation process includes all activities required to deploy the vendor's solution. Although the vendor will typically take the lead in managing this process, let's discuss the relevant issues surrounding design, development, testing, and deployment of the solution.

After discussing the Implementation process, this chapter discusses the people involved in this phase: the internal implementation team and the vendor implementation team. The information provided for the internal implementation team focuses on who the members are, what their roles are, and how they can make the implementation successful. The information provided for the vendor implementation team focuses on the role that the vendor's team plays in implementing the product.

THE IMPLEMENTATION PROCESS

The Implementation process consists of four potential subprocesses: design, development, testing, and deployment (Figure 6-1).

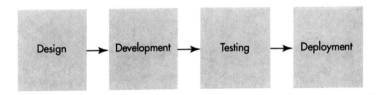

Figure 6-1: Implementation subprocesses

Before starting development, you need to define what will be developed, if anything. It is rare that you will be able to purchase technology and implement it as is. There is typically some customization, integration, and data conversion required for the new solution. The changes are defined in the design process.

Development includes all work needed to create or build the changes required for the new solution.

Once the vendor delivers the solution, you need to thoroughly test the solution. This includes system testing, user testing, and potentially pilot testing.

After passing the testing process, the solution needs to be deployed to the users. Training, deployment, and deployment support are discussed in the "Deployment" section later in this chapter.

Design

Chances are, the vendor's product will not meet 100 percent of your requirements. Normally, the vendor will agree to customize its product to meet your requirements in order to secure your business.

Once these changes are made, the vendor needs to work with you to integrate the solution within your environment and with other systems within your business.

If you have followed the acquisition process described in previous chapters, you will have thoroughly defined your requirements in the Planning phase. In the Implementation phase, you need to scrutinize the vendor's product and define any gaps between the vendor's product and your requirements. Once these gaps have been identified, you need to determine which ones are critical to your business. You also need to rely on your business analysts to tell you which gaps need to be resolved immediately and which ones can be deferred to a later time.

It is also a good idea to prioritize these requirement gaps so that the vendor works on the most important gaps first. You might need to define the requirements in greater detail in order for the vendor to understand what you are asking for. I recommend that you define the process down to a very detailed level and clearly define the functionality required to perform the activities within the process.

During the design process, the changes required to close the gaps need to be designed. This design informs developers how to modify the solution to close the gaps. It's a good idea to work with the vendor to document the design for architecture, process, data, application, and integration components of the solution. The technical analysts on your project team and the vendor's implementation team should know what is needed in order to document the design of the solution.

Development

In some technology acquisitions, there may come a time when you find you are tracking multiple gaps with multiple vendors. In this case, it is a good idea to develop a database to help track the changes. The database will help you organize priority, status, and ownership of all the product change requests that are being managed.

You should know which of your current systems needs to be integrated with the new system because you will have defined the system integration requirements during the Planning phase. At this time, you actually need to develop the integration between the systems. This may involve developing batch jobs or real-time updates between systems. Regardless of the ways in which you need to integrate the new system, you should plan for this development in advance and be ready to dedicate the resources necessary to properly integrate the new product within your environment.

Testing

Testing includes all activities required to verify the quality and capability of the solution. Testing is not as critical when buying technology as it is when building it. Vendors will thoroughly test their solutions, and in most cases, the product will have been successfully implemented at several other companies beforehand. In this case, your primary goal is to test the components that are unique to your environment. This includes testing the solution's compatibility, customizations, interfaces with other systems, performance, user acceptance, and results in a pilot test if necessary. There are several different types of tests that can be performed:

- *System testing:* The process of testing the solution within your environment to verify compatibility, performance, interfaces with other systems, and impact to the environment. These tests are typically conducted by your internal IT organization. The emphasis in these tests is on the technology and technical architecture, not the functionality.

- *User testing:* The process of users testing the solution for acceptance of functionality and usability. These tests are conducted by the end user of the solution and are typically facilitated by the IT organization. There are two types of user testing: vertical and horizontal. Vertical testing involves the testing of each group of functionality separately. Horizontal testing, on the other hand, involves the testing of the business processes (also referred to as end-to-end testing). I highly recommend that you exercise both forms of user testing.

  You should also consider managing user perception. The last thing you need is users testing the solution and then going back to their organizations and talking down the solution. To avoid this, get their commitment to allow the project team to work through any issues that the users identify and not to talk outside the testing team about the solution until the project team has had a fair chance to resolve those issues. User acceptance is often required prior to the deployment of the solution.

- *Pilot testing:* It is often a good idea to pilot test a vendor's solution before deploying it across the users' organization. A pilot test is a limited deployment of the solution in a production environment. This test provides a last chance to ensure that the solution is ready for full deployment.

Deployment

The deployment process verifies whether you made the right decision in selecting a quality vendor with a quality solution. You are now ready to deploy the solution into your production environment. This will be the true test of the new solution. Deploying a solution includes training, deployment, and deployment support.

Vendors typically offer some form of training. You should have learned about their training options during the Research phase. In some cases, the vendor will handle all training. In other cases, a vendor will outsource training to another company that specializes in training. And in most cases, the vendor will train your trainers and provide training materials (manuals, technology-based training, etc.).

The following case study discusses setting up testing environments.

Case Study

SEPARATING ENVIRONMENTS

XYZ Corporation used one environment for development, testing, and training. Once a product was ready, it was immediately moved into the production environment. One day there was a significant number of people in training, and the training environment crashed. Because XYZ Corporation was using one environment for development, testing, and training, all three were impacted by the crash. The developers didn't know about the training class, which resulted in the developers and testers spending several hours trying to figure out what happened to the environment. On the other side of the building, the training class was halted and eventually cancelled. This led to half a day of wasted man hours and poor user perception of the new system.

LESSON LEARNED
Always separate your development, testing, training, and production environments.

Once users are properly trained, deployment can begin. There are several ways to deploy a system. If there is an existing system, you may need to run both systems in parallel and slowly transition the users to the new system. In some cases, managing the integrity of the data between parallel systems is too costly, and it makes more sense to take everyone off the system at one time and bring them all up on the new system at the same time (commonly referred to as cut-over or go-live). Check with your vendor to see what it recommends. The vendor should have experience in deploying its solution in many different situations and should be able to recommend the approach that is appropriate for your situation.

Another important decision that needs to be made prior to deployment is who will support the system. Most companies have an internal support group that is responsible for supporting all information systems. This group should commit to providing a predetermined level of service and staffing the group appropriately. Typically, however, an internal support group will not have the bandwidth to support deployment of a new system. For this reason, it is often necessary to create a deployment support team. This is a temporary team that will assist in supporting the new solution until the system is completely deployed and has become stabilized.

The following checklist is provided as an aid to help you complete the tasks necessary for the Implementation process.

IMPLEMENTATION PROCESS CHECKLIST

❑ *The gaps between your requirements and the vendor's base product have been clearly defined, designed, and prioritized.*

❑ *The vendor has developed the functionality to close the gaps.*

❑ *The vendor has tested and delivered the product.*

❑ *The IT group has thoroughly system tested the product.*

❑ *The end user has tested and accepted the product.*

❑ *End users have been trained appropriately.*

❑ *The product has been deployed.*

THE INTERNAL IMPLEMENTATION TEAM

The internal implementation team is responsible for managing and executing the implementation of the system. This includes all activities that take place from the time the contracts are signed to the time that the system is fully operational and support is transitioned to the operations organization.

The internal implementation team is responsible for working with the vendor to support the vendor's efforts to implement its solution within the organization. This typically requires the following roles to be assigned:

- *Implementation project manager:* This individual is responsible for managing the internal implementation team and working with the vendor's project manager to coordinate implementation activities. Typically, the project manager manages the whole technology acquisition project from Initiation to Operations. In some cases, it is effective to have a project manager who specializes in managing technology acquisitions manage the project up to the point when the contracts are signed. The project manager then transitions management of the project to a business subject matter expert (SME). The SME coordinates training, deployment, and deployment support for the business organization. Because the vendor takes the lead in managing the deployment, the role of the SME mainly consists of being a liaison to the internal organization and helping to coordinate activities and resources.

- *Trainers:* Trainers are responsible for training the end users. In some organizations, there is a training department that handles all training programs. In other organizations where there isn't a training organization, some of the more experienced end users are assigned to this role. It is important that the trainers be positive and optimistic about the new solution. If they are negative about the new solution in any way, the trainees are likely to follow suit and have a bad opinion of the system.

- *Technical analysts:* If the new solution requires custom development or integration with other systems, there should be technical analysts on the internal implementation team. These analysts are responsible for designing the custom development and coordinating the development activities with their internal IT departments.

- *Testers:* Some organizations assign end users to the internal implementation team as full-time resources. Other organizations temporarily pull end users from their jobs to test a particular version of the system, and then send them back to their jobs when testing is finished. It is important to get a wide variety of end users involved in testing, from novice to experienced end users.

- *Deployment support:* As described earlier, a team is often set up to support the deployment. This team commonly consists of the business SMEs who have been on the project team from the beginning of the project. It is important that the deployment support people be the most educated about the vendor solution. Some vendors offer training for these individuals. Other vendors have their own personnel join the deployment support team to help educate the team and relate issues back to the vendor's development organization.

When implementing a new solution, it is important to have several respected individuals championing the cause within their own organizations. It is easier for these people to rally support for the new system when they are already respected. This is why I recommend that the initial project team of business SMEs stay with the project through the deployment process. They will gain an invaluable education on the vendor's solution during the Research phase and will have some ownership in the success of the project. Taking the time to cultivate these people into change leaders will increase your likelihood of a successful implementation.

THE VENDOR IMPLEMENTATION TEAM

Once contracts are signed and implementation is scheduled to begin, the vendor will assign a project team whose primary job is to implement the vendor's solution. The team members should have experience and know exactly what it takes to successfully implement their solution. It is a good idea to establish good working relationships between your internal implementation team and the vendor's implementation team as early as possible. This will ensure a good transfer of knowledge and teamwork in overcoming obstacles. The vendor's internal implementation team typically consists of the following roles:

- *Vendor project manager:* This senior person is responsible for planning, controlling, and executing all activities required to implement the vendor's solution. The project manager's experience in maneuvering a project through an external organization is invaluable. He will be able to steer the project clear of common mistakes and will have a better understanding of when a project is in trouble. Make sure that the vendor project manager has a point of contact in your organization who can help coordinate activities and resources within your organization. The project manager should also have a clear escalation path within your organization for issues that need a timely resolution.

- *Technical lead:* A technical lead needs to act as a liaison between your company and the vendor's development organization. This person is typically a senior person from the development organization who has a very deep understanding of the technology and how it was developed.

- *Developers:* Vendors often assign developers to a project team when a significant amount of custom development is required. These developers will have a wide variety of experience and expertise. It is the vendor's job to manage these developers and make sure that they are capable of accomplishing the task at hand.

- *Support analysts:* Vendors typically assign one or more support analysts to act as the liaison between your internal support organization and the vendor's support organization. The support analysts also play a role in supporting the deployment support team during the deployment of the system.

- *Trainers:* Trainers are responsible for either training your end users directly or training your trainers. In either case, these people will be responsible for educating your company about the vendor's solution.

It is important to ensure that a smooth hand-off takes place from the vendor's sales team to the vendor's implementation team. The promises made by the vendor's sales team need to be communicated to the implementation team, so that it can live up to those promises. It is a good idea to schedule an implementation kick-off meeting between the acquisition and implementation teams from both the vendor's and your organization. In this meeting, review all project documentation to ensure that everyone understands the expectations of what will be implemented and how.

7

Operation

Once the system has been successfully implemented, it is time to operate the system. The Operations phase consists of all on-going activities required to keep the system running smoothly for the lifetime of the solution.

In this chapter, the Operations process is discussed including managing fixes and enhancements to the vendor's solution and closing the project.

The people involved in the internal support team, vendor support team, and end user groups are also discussed.

THE OPERATIONS PROCESS

The Operations process consists of three potential subprocesses: fixes and enhancements, support, and project closure (Figure 7-1).

Once the vendor's solution is fully implemented, it is necessary to have a process in place for managing change requests for fixes and enhancements to the system. There is also a need for support processes to ensure that issues are resolved efficiently and effectively. The last process in the technology acquisition

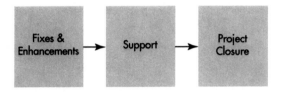

Figure 7-1: Operation subprocesses

project is to close the project. All of these topics are discussed throughout this chapter.

Fixes and Enhancements

How will you manage the process of requesting changes to the vendor's solution once it has been implemented? The project team will move on to other projects and will no longer be available to communicate and manage these changes with the vendor's development organization. You need to clearly define these processes so that changes will be addressed in an acceptable manner.

Vendors will often have processes in place to handle these change requests. In this case, it is just a matter of the vendor educating your team on its process. Some companies prefer to use their own change request process and require all of their vendors to support their process. If this is the case, make sure you communicate this requirement to the vendor early in the technology acquisition project. This will prevent the vendor from resisting this prerequisite later in the project when it already has your business.

Regardless of whose process is used, it is important that the process be clearly documented with ownership and accountability built in throughout the process. Place time expectations on each activity in the process. If these times are exceeded, make sure you have an escalation process defined as well. Taking the time to define these processes will minimize confusion and improve consistency in dealing with the vendor effectively.

Support

What will happen if there is an issue with the operation of the vendor's solution? Will end users contact your support group or the vendor's support group? These are some of the questions that need to be answered prior to deployment of the solution.

Define the process that an issue will go through from identification to resolution. This may include a call to your internal help desk and then escalate to the vendor's help desk to resolve the issue. On the other hand, you may decide to have the end users contact the vendor's help desk directly when an issue arises. In either case, you should have a clear process and a way of measuring the performance of that process.

You will also need to define the issue escalation process. What happens when the whole system is down? Who gets paged during working hours, and who gets paged during nonworking hours? If the vendor is supporting the solution directly with the end users, at what point should the vendor notify you of a severe issue? Take the time to define which issues should be escalated and to whom, so that you and the vendor can react quickly in the event of a disaster.

Project Closure

When should a project end? This is not always as easy to answer as it may seem. There will come a time when the system has been implemented, and the project teams are working to resolve issues. At some point, it is appropriate to hand off management of these issues to the support organizations and dissolve the project teams and deployment support teams. Determining exactly when you have reached this point is a judgement call. Generally speaking, it is time to close the project when all of the project objectives have been met. The problem with this determination is that it is not cost-effective for the project team to remain on the project until 100 percent of the objectives are met. Typically, a project is closed when between 80-100 percent of the objectives are met.

When approaching the time to close the project, it is important to close it properly. The following activities are necessary to properly close a project:

- *Project documentation:* Assemble all project documentation into a project notebook. Physically, this can be a binder, a series of binders, or a network drive where all project documentation will reside. This binder should be the primary source of documentation for the acquisition portion of the project after the acquisition is complete. Most organizations have a library where this type of documentation resides. There are many benefits to ensuring clear documentation of the project including the following:

- *Supports the decision:* It is inevitable that someone, at some point, will question the decision that has been made. Having thorough documentation of the process that was undertaken will support the decision and help people understand why the chosen vendor was best for the given situation.

• *Provides a great source of education:* Future technology acquisition project managers will benefit from reading through the documentation and gaining an understanding of what worked well and what didn't. Project documentation will help your organization start to capture a set of best practices in technology acquisition project management.

• *Accountability:* Project documentation clearly documents the expectations of what the business needs are and what the vendor has promised to provide. These terms can change if they are passed from person to person as verbal communication. The result can be a misinterpretation of what is expected of the vendor and what the vendor has promised to provide. Written documentation is the only way to ensure consistent communication of what was agreed to during the technology acquisition.

• *Insurance:* There is always the possibility that one party will not live up to its side of the agreement. This can result in litigation. No one likes to think about this possibility, but it does happen from time to time. Having clear documentation can be very beneficial in keeping litigation from taking place as well as in assisting your legal team during litigation if it comes to that.

• *Measure success:* If you defined how you would measure success in the project charter, it is time to take the final measurements to determine how successful the project was. Many people do a poor job of taking measurements prior to implementing the new solution. This makes it difficult to determine success at the end of the project. Taking the time to record measurements at the beginning and end of the implementation enables you to answer the question of whether the project was successful and support that answer with data.

• *Celebrate success:* Assuming the project was successful, it is necessary to celebrate your success as a team. This will help the team bring closure to the effort mentally and force you to take the time to think about what has been accomplished and what lessons were learned along the way. It is also a good idea to document the lessons learned. They can help others learn from your experiences in the future.

- *Resource evaluations:* Remember that your project team members have taken time away from their normal jobs and managers to help with the project. Their management has had minimal visibility of the type of work they have been involved in during this time. It is very important that the project manager closes the loop and evaluates each member of the project team. When finished, review the evaluation with the project team member and then with his or her manager. This will allow you to give credit where credit is due. Remember that you will be more likely to get the best people on your project teams if you have a reputation for rewarding good work.

- *Project closure processes:* Your organization may have formal processes in place for opening and closing projects. If this is the case, make sure you submit all documents that are required to close the project. Don't leave any loose ends or clutter for others to clean up at a later time.

- *Approvals:* The project sponsors have the final say in closing the project. The project manager needs their approval before the project can officially be closed and he can move on to other projects.

The following checklist is provided as an aid to help you complete the tasks necessary for the Operations process.

OPERATIONS PROCESS CHECKLIST

❑ *The process for requesting fixes and enhancements has been clearly defined and documented.*

❑ *The vendor has approved the process for managing fixes and enhancements.*

❑ *Support groups and processes are in place.*

❑ *End user support has been trained to adequately support the product.*

❑ *The end users know who to contact for support.*

❑ *All project documentation has been assembled into a project notebook.*

❑ *Lessons learned have been documented.*

❑ *The project has been officially closed.*

THE INTERNAL SUPPORT TEAM

Your internal support team consists of all organizations that are responsible for maintaining the system for the duration of its use. There are typically two general types of support: end user support and operational support.

End User Support

End user support is the first line of support for end users when they experience issues with the new system. End users will usually have a telephone hotline to call for help. Often, there are several levels of support within the end user support organization. The first level support people answer the phones and resolve common issues. If first level support people cannot resolve the issue, they escalate the call to a second level of support. This level usually consists of the senior support people who are more knowledgeable and experienced with the systems. If the second level support people cannot resolve the issue, they usually escalate the issue to the vendor's support organization. The vendor's support people then track the issue to resolution and respond to the end user with progress updates.

In some cases, it may make sense to have the vendor support the end user directly. In this case, users would still call a telephone hotline, but they would be talking to a first level support person in the vendor's organization. If the solution requires a physical visit, the vendor can escalate a call to your internal support organization. Be sure to iron out the details during the Research, Evaluation, and Negotiation processes about who will support the end users once the solution is implemented.

When setting up a support program, you should define the service level requirements. For example, you should specify whether the solution requires 24 x 7 support or only standard business-hour support. Additionally, you should define the response time expectations. For example, you might require that all calls be answered within 30 seconds. All issues should be assigned a tracking number. Issues that cannot be resolved should be escalated to a second level of support with a response back to the user within 24 hours. All of the requirements that define the level of service required are called *Service Level Agreements (SLAs)*.

If you decide to support the end users with your internal support organization, you should plan for training of that organization. Vendors often provide advanced training courses for technical people. These training programs educate them on the solution and provide them with the information required for providing effective support. Find out if the vendor offers this type of training during the Research process. If the vendor does not, try to get the internal support group members involved in the project as early in the Implementation process as possible so that they will have adequate time to learn the system.

As discussed earlier, when to transition support from the deployment support team to the end user support organization is not always apparent. Integrating the end user support organization into the deployment support team will enable a smooth transition.

Operational Support

Most companies have an internal organization that is responsible for managing and maintaining the technical environment. Although this organization can have many different names, let's call it the operational support department for the purposes of this book. This organization is responsible for the following tasks after the implementation of the new solution:

- *Routine backups:* The operational support department should have a full backup of the system scheduled on a regular basis. The frequency will be determined by the criticality of the data in the system.

- *Disaster recovery:* There should always be a disaster recovery plan in place for each system required to run the business. In an emergency, the operational support department is responsible for launching the execution of the disaster recovery plan.

- *Monitoring:* Operational personnel monitor the environment. This ensures stability and identifies issues quickly. Monitoring can include servers, databases, or interfaces between systems.

- *Maintenance:* Some systems require a little maintenance to keep them running smoothly. For example, operational personnel may need to clear out log files or recycle a server on a regular basis in order to maintain the system.

- *Processing:* Some processes need to be initiated manually. For example, backing up the system may require a person to manually switch tapes between backups. These processes are typically initiated by the operational support organization. Another process could be a batch process to move data between two systems.

Just as you need to train the end user support organization to support the new system, you also need to train the operational support group. In most cases, this will not require significant training because you will be trying to acquire a system that fits nicely into your existing environment. Training will consist more of these individuals learning the processes of setting up and configuring the new solution. The vendor should play a significant role in training the operational support group.

THE VENDOR SUPPORT TEAM

Initially in the acquisition project, there is a vendor sales team. Once the sales process has been completed, the project is transitioned over to a vendor implementation team. This team is responsible for implementing the solution in your business. The final transition in this process is from the vendor implementation team to the vendor support team. The vendor support team is responsible for managing the ongoing relationship with your business. This team provides the following:

- *Product support:* Vendors almost always provide some form of support for their products. This may be in the form of direct end user support, second- or third-level support for the customer's support organization, or support via electronic means such as e-mail or discussion boards. Make sure your Research process defines the type of support that will be offered by the vendor after the solution is implemented.

- *Product changes:* Vendors will customize their products upon request, usually with a fee attached, or fix defects in their products on an ongoing basis. These changes are usually bundled into a product release in approximately six-month intervals. Find out how often the vendor delivers new releases and what the process is to request a change to the product.

- *Training:* You should plan for ongoing training support from the vendor. This may be in the form of training, training of trainers, technology-based training, or training manuals. Regardless of which methods are employed to train your end users, you will inevitably need to provide ongoing training for new staff members.

- *User groups:* Some vendors coordinate activities for a user group of their customers. Vendors provide funding for efforts that build community between their customers. This is a win-win situation for vendors and their customers. Vendors can invite prospects, giving their customers a chance to sell their product for them. On the other hand, the peer relationships that can develop between customers can be invaluable in sharing ideas and

discussing solutions to common issues surrounding a vendor's solution.
Find out if your vendors have user groups for their customers.

These are just some of the services that a vendor support organization can provide. It is important to negotiate the level of service that a vendor will provide prior to signing the contracts. Waiting until the solution is completely implemented in your business before discussing service levels puts you in a weaker position to demand increases in service offerings. As mentioned earlier, these predefined minimum levels of service are typically called SLAs. Make sure the vendor has a clear understanding of what your expectations are in terms of level of service provided.

It is also important to monitor the vendor's service and support periodically. Define a set schedule for reviewing the status of the solution and relationship on a biannual or annual basis. This review should include key members of the vendor's staff. In this meeting, you should review everything that has happened since the implementation of the solution, changes that are required, and strategic planning for future use of the vendor's technology.

The last point that I want to stress in dealing with the vendor's support organization is to maintain good communications with the vendor. This means keeping the vendor up-to-date on the changes and challenges taking place in your business and asking the vendor to do the same. It may even include helping the vendor plan its future offerings. It is important to remember that the vendor is your technology partner and will only be successful if you are successful and possibly vice versa.

THE END USER

It is important that the end users of the solution are adequately represented on the project team and internal implementation team. If you don't have the support of the end users and the solution doesn't meet their requirements, it will be difficult for the solution to be successful. The project sponsor should take the time at the beginning of the project to campaign for support from the end users' management staff. This will ensure that there is support from the end user organization throughout the project.

Also, you should think about how to generate interest in the new solution. I have seen posters, mouse pads, T-shirts, flyers, coffee mugs, pens, key chains, and even videos demonstrating the benefits of the new solution. The method is not as important as the message that is communicated. Let the users know what life will be like with the new solution so that they have some time to get used to the new changes. This will inspire them to participate in training and hopefully to embrace the new solution once it is implemented. One thing I will caution you about is not to communicate this information too early. I have seen project managers place posters, mouse pads, and flyers all over their company only to experience extreme delays in implementing the solution. This was a waste of money because the communication was required again once the solution was actually ready for deployment. It also created a negative impression of the system within the user community. End users would roll their eyes whenever someone mentioned that the new solution would solve one of their problems. Be careful to communicate relevant information only when you are sure the solution is ready, and then go overboard and do it right.

Once the new solution is deployed, you are likely to experience some resistance to change by the end users. In a previous call-tracking system deployment, I had a manager say that the users would scream about not being able to do their jobs because of the new system; then, within six months they would be screaming every time it went down saying that they can't do their jobs without it. He was absolutely right. The users resisted and did everything they could to stop the implementation, stating that it slowed them down too much to track calls. Eight months later, we were sitting in a meeting getting chewed out by the end user management because the system was down for an hour and the users couldn't do their jobs without it. This is when you know that you were successful. Keep in mind that everyone has a different rate of accepting change. It is inevitable that there will be resistance to the change initially, but be persistent, and eventually the end users will accept and embrace the new solution.

There you have it! You have now walked through a process that has been used successfully in several technology acquisition projects at Fortune 1,000 companies. You have also learned about the different groups of people involved in the process.

As I stated in the Introduction, the purpose of this book is to get you through your first technology acquisition project. For this reason, I tried to keep the process as linear and as simple as possible while still producing a quality decision. Now it's time to advance the topic of technology acquisition project management. Join me at www.technologyacquisition.com and share your experiences in managing this type of project. On this Web site, you will find papers on hot topics, discussion groups, and a free monthly e-mail newsletter. You can also read more about my books, articles, workbooks, keynotes, and audio/video products.

I wish you success in your first technology acquisition project and many more to come.

Resources

Books

Steinberg, Leigh. *Winning with Integrity.* Villard Books, New York, NY: 1998. This is a great book on the art of negotiating.

McConnell, Steve. *Rapid Development.* Microsoft Press, Redmond, WA: 1996. This is an invaluable book on software project management and a great reference for your bookshelf at work.

Project Management Institute. *A Guide to the Project Management Body of Knowledge 2000.* Project Management Institute, Newtown Square, PA: 2001. This book is the primary source of generally accepted project management practices. The Project Management Institute provides a certification based on the information in this book.

Web Sites

Allen Eskelin (www.alleneskelin.com) or (www.technologyacquisition.com): My personal Web site which includes monthly hot topics and a free e-mail newsletter.

Project Management Institute (www.pmi.org): The PMI Web site includes information on its certification programs and annual project management conference.

ALLPM (www.allpm.com): ALLPM is a good project management Web site with an extensive library of resources on various topics related to project management.

Index

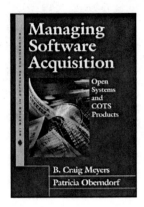

Managing Software Acquisition
Open Systems and COTS Products
By B. Craig Meyers and Patricia Oberndorf
SEI Series in Software Engineering

The acquisition of open systems and commercial off-the-shelf (COTS) products is an increasingly vital part of large-scale software development, offering significant savings in time and money. This book presents fundamental principles and best practices for successful acquisition and utilization of open systems and COTS products.

0-201-70454-4 • Hardcover • 400 pages • ©2001

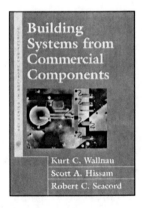

Building Systems from Commercial Components
Kurt C. Wallnau, Scott A. Hissam, and Robert C. Seacord
SEI Series in Software Engineering

Commercial components are increasingly seen as an effective means to save time and money in building large software systems. However, integrating pre-existing components, with pre-existing specifications, is a delicate and difficult task. This book describes specific engineering practices needed to accomplish that task successfully, illustrating the techniques described with case studies and examples.

0-201-70064-6 • Hardcover • 416 pages • ©2002

Component-Based Software Engineering
Putting the Pieces Together
By George T. Heineman and William T. Councill

This book provides a comprehensive overview of, and current perspectives on, component-based software engineering (CBSE). With contributions from well-known luminaries in the field, it defines what CBSE really is, details CBSE's benefits and pitfalls, describes CBSE experiences from around the world, and ultimately reveals CBSE's considerable potential for engineering reliable and cost-effective software.

0-201-70485-4 • Hardcover • 880 pages • ©2001

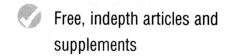
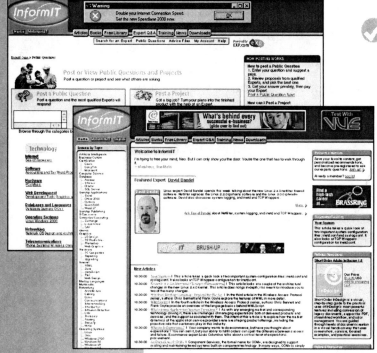 

CPSIA information can be obtained at www.ICGtesting.com
Printed in the USA
LVOW11s1026280813

350004LV00005B/75/P